The Mexican Texans

W9-CPB-847

DATE DUE

APR 1 4 2014

TEXANS ALL

A Series from
the Institute of Texan Cultures
Sara R. Massey, General Editor

The Mexican Texans

Phyllis McKenzie

TEXAS A&M UNIVERSITY PRESS ❧ COLLEGE STATION

The Ellwood Foundation, Houston, Texas, provided funding
support for the research and writing of this book.

The paper used in this book meets the minimum requirements
of the American National Standard for Permanence
of Paper for Printed Library Materials, z39.48-1984.
Binding materials have been chosen for durability.

Illustrations on title page and chapter heads are details
from the map by Jack Jackson found on page 2.

LIBRARY OF CONGRESS CATALOGING-IN-PUBLICATION DATA

McKenzie, Phyllis, 1957–

    The Mexican Texans / Phyllis McKenzie.—1st ed.

        p. cm.—(Texans all)

    Includes bibliographical references and index.

    ISBN 1-58544-306-9 (cloth : alk. paper)—

    ISBN 1-58544-307-7 (pbk. : alk. paper)

    1. Mexican Americans—Texas—History. 2. Mexican Americans—Texas—
Social life and customs. 3. Mexican Americans—Texas—Ethnic identity.
4. Immigrants—Texas—History. 5. Texas—History. 6. Texas—Ethnic relations.
7. Texas—Relations—Mexico. 8. Mexico—Relations—Texas. I. University of Texas
Institute of Texan Cultures at San Antonio. II. Title. III. Series.

F395.M5M38   2004

976.4'0046872—dc22   2003016356

Contents

Illustrations

Foreword

The Institute of Texan Cultures opened in 1968 with exhibits depicting the cultural groups that settled early Texas. The displays resulted from a massive research effort by many young scholars into the history of Texas. This research served as the basis for writing what became known as "the ethnic pamphlet series." The series included pamphlets devoted to the Swiss Texans, the Norwegian Texans, the Native American Texans, the Mexican Texans, the Greek Texans, the Spanish Texans, the African American Texans, the Chinese Texans, and many more. Some years later several books about additional cultural groups were produced, including the Japanese Texans, the Irish Texans, the Polish Texans, and numerous others.

Thirty years later, as staff reviewed the early pamphlets, they realized that although the material remained accurate, it was time for a revision of the series, along with a fresh look. Thus emerged the new book set, Texans All. Organized by world regions, each volume summarizes and provides examples of the social and cultural contributions made by the major groups immigrating to Texas rather than the traditional historical chronologies that focused on politics, wars, and great men. The book set includes the five distinctive cultural groups that already existed in Texas prior to its statehood or that came to Texas in the early twentieth century: *The Indian Texans, The Mexican Texans, The European Texans, The African Texans,* and *The Asian Texans.*

The author of each book used an organizational pattern dictated by the content. (*The Mexican Texans* is organized chronologically, for instance.) The authors have additionally searched for primary sources to incorporate within the text, and sidebars provide additional biographical or topical sketches. As the manuscripts neared completion, maps were commissioned to illustrate the settlement areas of the various cultural groups in nineteenth-century Texas. But as the various groups adapted to the land and culture of others and new generations were born, their separate cultural identities began to merge with others, and the ethnic origins of many communities faded. With the exodus from rural communities to larger towns and cities in the early twentieth century, the unique cultural identity of rural communities further blurred.

Many of the people presented in words and photographs will be unknown, since most of the stories are about ordinary people who struggled to build a home and make a living in Texas. The majority of the more than three hundred photographs used in this book set are from the Institute of Texan Cultures Research Library's extensive photograph collection of over three million images relating to the people of Texas.

The Mexican Texans is a sweeping saga about the blending of people from Spain and Mexico who eventually moved north into what became Texas. It is a story of a peoples' struggle that began on the frontier and continues into the environment of the twenty-first century. Many of the descendants of the early Mexican families still live in Texas as sixth- and seventh-generation Texans. Cultural legacies from the early years persist and add to the uniqueness that is Texas.

New immigrants arriving from Mexico continue to renew and reenergize Tejano communities with their sustaining religious values, folk medicines, music, language, and customs. The continuity of Mexican culture in Texas over the decades has enriched the lives of all that are touched by the generosity and spirit of a people.

Vivan los mexicanos!

Sara R. Massey

The Mexican Texans

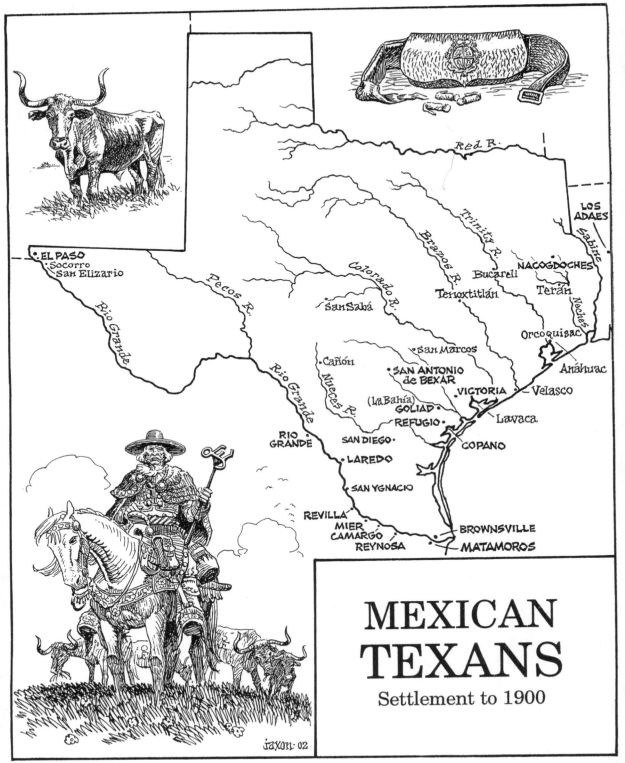

Labels on map:

Red R.

LOS ADAES

Trinity R.

Brazos R.

Bucareli

NACOGDOCHES

Terán

Sabine

Tenoxtitlán

Neches

EL PASO
Socorro
San Elizario

Pecos R.

Colorado R.

San Sabá

Orcoquisac

San Marcos

Anáhuac

Rio Grande

Cañón

SAN ANTONIO
de BEXAR

VICTORIA

Velasco

Nueces R.

(La Bahía)
GOLIAD

Lavaca

Rio Grande

REFUGIO

COPANO

RIO
GRANDE

SAN DIEGO

LAREDO

SAN YGNACIO

REVILLA
MIER
CAMARGO
REYNOSA

BROWNSVILLE
MATAMOROS

MEXICAN
TEXANS

Settlement to 1900

Jaxon-02

Mexican Texan settlement up to 1900. Map by Jack Jackson

Introduction

Mexican Texans have a complex identity. They encompass people who call themselves *tejanos, mexicanos, indígenas, latinos,* Latin Americans, Mexican Americans, Hispanics, and more. The Mexican aspect of identity is equally complex—a blending of Spanish and indigenous cultures with additions from elsewhere including Moorish Africa. Mexican philosopher José Vasconcelos described the mingling of races in Mexico as the origin of a "cosmic race."[1]

People migrated north from Mexico over many different time periods to the northern frontier of New Spain, which later became Texas. Some stayed, settled, raised families, and made Texas their permanent home. In some cases, six and seven generations of their descendants have lived on the same land. They preserved elements of their Mexican culture while adapting to new conditions and initiating changes.

Spain claimed the area for over three centuries. During this long era, adventurers, soldiers, settlers, and priests streamed north from Mexico to Texas. They eked out a living in frontier conditions, formed alliances with native peoples, and created communities to address their needs. The Spanish colonial era sowed the seeds of a distinct identity in Texas. As soon as they arrived, the newcomers began to interact and blend with the native people, or *indios*. Their descendants became the Mexican Texans of today.

CHAPTER 1

Establishing Roots

The Colonial Era, 1519–1821

*I*N 1519 SPANIARD Hernán Cortés docked his ship on the coast of Mexico near present-day Veracruz. He heard reports of a huge city in the interior—Tenochtitlán, seat of the Aztec empire. Cortés marched inland with a few hundred soldiers and an Indian woman to guide them. Along the way they met natives who were unhappy with Aztec rule. Cortés made alliances with these Indian bands and continued onward. Reaching Tenochtitlán, the troops gazed in wonder at long causeways that linked an island city to shores of a lake. They marveled at elaborate art made of gold, jade, and feathers. Tenochtitlán, home to 250,000 residents, was the largest city in the world at that time.

At first, the Aztec emperor Montezuma welcomed the Spaniards. He believed Cortés was the long-lost god Quetzalcoatl, who had sailed east many years before with the promise to return one day. Then smallpox and other European diseases struck the Aztecs, killing thousands. Survivors began to distrust the intentions of their uninvited guests. Rallying their forces, the Aztecs drove the intruders from the city. However, the Spaniards soon returned with their Indian allies. Cortés and his band imprisoned the emperor and killed his successor. When the Spaniards built Mexico City over the ruins of Tenochtitlán, the empire of New Spain was born.

yliyocan.

An Indian view of the Spanish Conquest from the codex of Lienzo de Tlaxcala, sixteenth century. Institute of Texan Cultures illustration nos. 68-2096 and 68-2010

THE AZTECS AND AZTLÁN. Despite the wealth of their capital city, the Aztecs had not lived in the region for long. They arrived in central Mexico perhaps two hundred years before the Spaniards. According to legend, their original home had been a place to the northwest called Aztlán. After years of wandering and suffering, the exiles spotted an eagle holding a snake in its beak. The eagle showed them where to build their city on an island in the lake. This eagle image appears on the flag of modern Mexico to honor its Aztec roots.

Some scholars believe the Aztecs began their migration from an area that is now the southwestern United States. During the Chicano movement of the 1970s, the oral tradition of Aztlán became a rallying point for Mexican Americans. As one young woman wrote, "It is especially ignorant for someone to say that Mexican Americans should go back where we came from. The U.S. Southwest *is* where we are from."[1]

SPANISH IMPERIAL POLICY. After Cortés had destroyed the power of the Aztecs, Spain laid claim to vast territories. Francisco Pizarro, also from Spain, conducted a similar conquest of the Inca in Peru. The Spanish crown set up two administrative centers, one in New Spain (Mexico) and one in Peru. A viceroy was appointed to manage the affairs of each region. Spanish administrators believed the purpose of colonies was to profit the mother country. They melted down irreplaceable ancient art into gold bars and shipped them to Spain.

A number of Spanish adventurers tried to repeat the successes of Cortés and Pizarro, but they never again found dazzling cities like those of the Aztec and Inca. Mexico's greatest resources lay in silver and fertile lands rather than in gold. To develop this potential for wealth, officials turned to the native people.

Spain established a feudal system of land ownership. Indians provided the labor. In exchange, the Spanish overseers were responsible for protecting and instructing them. The Indians toiled in horrible conditions in the silver mines of northern Mexico. Almost immediately, individuals began to voice concern and protest the mistreatment of Indian people. In 1537 the pope declared people of the Americas to be human beings with souls. Despite the excesses of the era—including acts of greed and cruelty—most Spanish settlers were profoundly religious. Friars and priests journeyed throughout the New World with the sincere intent of saving souls.

THE VIRGIN OF GUADALUPE. Reports place the Virgin of Guadalupe in the Americas just ten years after the Spanish Conquest. Juan Diego, a poor Indian, described seeing the Virgin Mary next to the shrine of the Aztec mother goddess. The Virgin told him to have the bishop build a church for her there. As proof of her presence, she directed Juan to a nearby hill where he found roses blooming in the midwinter chill. Juan wrapped the blossoms in his cloak and carried them to the bishop. When they opened the cloth, they discovered that the Virgin's image had been miraculously formed on the inside of the cloth. The Virgin, like Juan and other New World Indians, had dark skin.

This story symbolizes the acceptance of Indians into the church and a blending of indigenous and Catholic beliefs. The Virgin of Guadalupe, Mexico's patron saint, has become a unifying image for Hispanics throughout the Americas.

MESTIZAJE (ETHNIC BLENDING). From the start of their occupation of Mexico, Spanish settlers married native women and fathered children by them. The government encouraged this practice, believing families would bring stability to the colony. Intermingling gave rise to a generation of *mestizos,* children born of one Spanish parent and one Indian parent.

Vulnerable to European diseases, large numbers of Indians died. The Indian population declined steeply while the numbers of mixed-blood inhabitants grew. About 90 percent of Mexicans living today are descended from both Spanish and Indian ancestors.

EXPLORATIONS IN TEXAS

During the sixteenth century, Spain financed several expeditions into the frontier north of Mexico City. The main goal of these explorations was to find gold, but they also served to map the territory, to learn about the inhabitants, and to strengthen Spanish claims to the area.

THE FIRST *ENTRADAS*. Alonso Álvarez de Pineda is the first known European to gaze upon the land that would become Texas. Instructed to find a sea route to the Orient, he scouted and mapped part of the Texas Gulf Coast in 1519, the same year that Cortés marched into the heart of the Aztec empire.

Nine years later, Álvar Núñez Cabeza de Vaca landed in Texas. He was a survivor of the ill-fated Narváez expedition, which had started overland in Florida and ended with men in wooden rafts desperately seeking a way home. Washed ashore on the Texas coast, Cabeza de Vaca and a few companions lived as slaves among Indians for a time. In 1536 they made their way through the South Texas brushland and succeeded in reaching Mexico City.

The next Spanish expedition was magnificently equipped and outfitted—even the horses wore armor. In 1540 Francisco Vásquez de Coronado set out from Mexico City to find the Seven Cities of Cíbola and, afterward, Quivira. Indians had described such towns to Cabeza de Vaca—fantastic places, they promised, gleaming in gold. Coronado pushed north through New Mexico and Texas, wandering east as far as Kansas, but found nothing except humble villages. Coronado's men were the first Europeans to cross the Texas Panhandle. They left a description of the Plains Indians, a people who had never before seen horses: "These people are called Querechos and Tejas. . . . They travel like the Arabs, with their tents and troops

Cabeza de Vaca, Texas Explorer

Cabeza de Vaca's odyssey through Florida, Texas, and Mexico is one of the greatest adventure tales in history. Born in Spain about 1490, Cabeza de Vaca sailed to the New World in 1527 under Pánfilo de Narváez, the commander in charge of Florida. At the time, geographers believed Florida was only a short distance from the shores of Mexico. Narváez's expedition set out to investigate the coastline but suffered swift losses from hurricanes, shipwrecks, and desertion. The remaining men patched together makeshift rafts by cutting planks and sealing the wood with pine resin. For sails they sacrificed their shirts.

More gulf storms followed. Cabeza de Vaca and a few others washed onto an island off the coast of Texas.

Title page to Cabeza de Vaca's Relación, *the first book about Texas, published in 1542. Institute of Texan Cultures illustration no. 68-2017*

of dogs loaded with poles. . . . They are a kind people and not cruel. They are faithful friends. They are able to make themselves very well understood by means of signs. They dry the flesh in the sun, cutting it thin as a leaf."[2]

THE ORIGINS OF TEXAS. The Panhandle tribe Tejas may have given rise to the name "Texas." More likely, the word comes from the Caddo Indian language. In 1689 Spanish troops surprised a Caddo settlement in eastern Texas. When the Indians fled into the woods, the soldiers' native guide followed and implored them to return. Describing the events, a Franciscan friar recalled, "He called to them, declaring that we were friends and that they should have no fear. Some of them—among these was their captain—came out and embraced us saying, 'Techas! Techas!' which means 'Friends! Friends!'"[3]

A pen-and-ink drawing of conquistadores by Thom Ricks. Institute of Texan Cultures illustration no. 82-14

Local Karankawa Indians received them kindly, but misfortune dogged the Spaniards. Hunger, cold weather, illness, squabbles, and misguided scouting trips reduced their numbers.

Cabeza de Vaca and three other survivors traveled inland, pushing south and southwest in search of home. For a time they worked as slaves under demanding Indian masters. Other native groups, in contrast, revered the Spaniards as healers. Cabeza de Vaca described their awe: "So great was the confidence that they would be healed if we administered to them, they even believed that while we remained none of them could die. . . ."

Cabeza de Vaca performed the first recorded surgery in North America by cutting an arrow from an Indian's chest and stitching the wound. He recorded the customs of the Indian groups he met, many of whom disappeared shortly after Spanish contact.

In 1535 Cabeza de Vaca and his companions spotted a group of mounted Spaniards in the distance. The vagabonds had finally reached northwest Mexico. A few years later Cabeza de Vaca published a vivid account of his experiences, stirring readers to dream of further explorations.

Sources: "The Narrative of Alvar Nuñez Cabeza de Vaca," in *Sanish Explorers in the Southern United States, 1528–1543*, ed. Frederick W. Hodge (1907; reprint, New York: Barnes & Noble, Inc., 1965), pp. 78, 101; Jack Lowry, "New World Odyssey," *Texas Highways* 39, no. 1 (Jan., 1992): 35–41.

Another possible origin for the word comes from María de Ágreda, a young nun in Spain during the 1620s. She declared that she had been transported to America several times while in a trance. In America she had met native people called Titlas, or Ticlas, and had spoken to them about God. María's priests discussed her remarkable travels with churchmen in New Spain. The men concluded that she might have visited the Jumano Indians of southwestern Texas.

In 1629, when Spaniards first met the Jumano, the Indians described a "Lady in Blue" who had appeared and taught them about Christianity. Many years later the East Texas Indians, the ones who had cried *"Techas"* in greeting, told a priest about a mysterious woman from the distant past. "The [Indian] Governor replied that they liked the color blue very much, especially for burial clothes, because in times past a very beautiful woman used to visit them, coming down from on high dressed in blue, and they wanted to be like her. . . . It is clear they were referring to Mother María de Jesús de Ágreda."[4]

A NEW THREAT TO SPANISH RULE. By 1600 authorities reluctantly concluded that Texas contained no treasures of silver or gold. For nearly a century, they showed little interest in funding new expeditions into the region. Spanish settlers in New Mexico sometimes traded with Jumano Indians, native merchants who traversed rugged terrain and served as middlemen to other Indians farther east. Then an expedition by France changed matters dramatically and rekindled Spain's interest in Texas.

In 1682, Robert Cavelier, Sieur de La Salle, reached the mouth of the Mississippi and claimed the river with all its tributaries for France. France and Spain were at war in Europe. La Salle proposed to King Louis XIV that France strengthen its claims in America by setting up a colony to trade with the Indians near the Mississippi River on the Gulf of Mexico. On his return voyage, he miscalculated his ships' position and landed in Texas rather than at the mouth of the Mississippi River. In 1685 the French settlers built Fort St. Louis near the Texas Gulf Coast.

▼▼▼

La V. M. Maria de Jesus de Agreda Predicanda à los Chichimecos del Nuebo-mexico. Ant.º de Caso f.

A seventeenth-century woodcut of María de Jesús de Ágreda. Institute of Texan Cultures illustration no. 68-2021

Hearing word of the French enemy in its territory, Spain took swift action. The government dispatched five expeditions by sea and four by land to locate the French. All efforts failed until 1689, when Alonso de León found only forlorn ruins at the site of the fort. "We . . . found all the houses sacked, all the chests, bottle cases and all the

▼▼▼

La Salle's landing on the Texas coast, from a book published in London in 1698. Institute of Texan Cultures illustration no. 72-69

rest of the settlers' furniture broken; apparently more than two hundred books, torn apart, with the rotten leaves scattered through the patios—all in French. . . . The houses are of stakes, covered with mud inside and out; their roofs are covered with buffalo hides. All are quite useless for any defense."[5]

The Spaniards provided a Christian burial for the bodies they

▼▼▼

found. De León reported that the settlement posed no threat to Spain. However, the Spanish government concluded it must occupy Texas to stop other countries from claiming the territory.

SETTLING TEXAS

BEGINNINGS AND SETTLEMENT PLANS. By the end of the seventeenth century, outposts already existed within the boundaries of the future state of Texas. El Paso had been known as a favorable place to cross the Rio Grande since the Oñate expedition of 1598. In 1680 New Mexico Indians fleeing the Pueblo Revolt gathered to build the Ysleta and Socorro Missions near El Paso.

Mapmakers placed these western settlements inside the Spanish province of Nuevo León. Texas was a vast and wild region to the east, stretching to a vague boundary with French Louisiana. Spain claimed this territory as the Province of Texas and appointed a governor in 1691.

In 1690 Alonso de León, accompanied by a Catholic priest, made

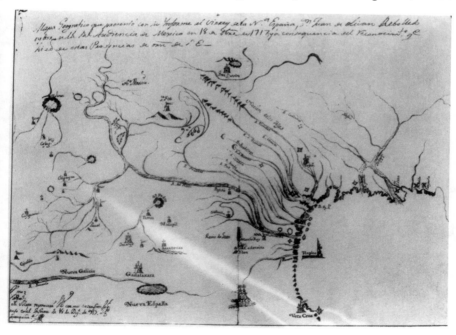

Spanish map of Texas in 1717, showing San Francisco de los Tejas and other missions. Institute of Texan Cultures illustration no. 71-52

his fifth and final expedition into Texas. These resolute Spaniards proceeded northeast toward the French borderlands and built the first mission that was indisputably on Texas soil, San Francisco de los Tejas. On his journey, De León gave names to the rivers that are still used today: the Nueces, Frio, Medina, and Guadalupe.

Unfortunately, only a few soldiers stayed behind to defend the new mission. The woodland Indians proved to be reluctant converts, especially when disease fell upon them. They feared that if they agreed to be baptized, the ceremonial water would kill them. Suffering from a lack of supplies, Mission San Francisco closed its doors within three years.

Funeral procession for a fever victim at Mission San Francisco de los Tejas, 1691. From Carlos Castañeda's Our Catholic Heritage in Texas, *published in 1936.* Institute of Texan Cultures illustration no. 71-58

Despite the setback at Mission San Francisco, missions soon dotted Spanish Texas. Authorities established new ones toward the south, along the central Rio Grande in 1700. This time they added forts for protection, realizing military assistance was vital if they were to survive. Administrators called for a network of settlements that would include missions *(misiones)* to instruct the Indians, forts

(*presidios*) to protect them, and civilian towns (*villas*) for families to build a community.

A few years later reports surfaced of renewed French activity. French frontiersmen had made contact and begun trading with Indians along the Louisiana-Texas border. Receiving these reports, Spain promptly established a string of six missions, including a reincarnation of Mission San Francisco, and a fort in northeast Texas.

Issuing a new alarm, an inspector pleaded for fortifications on the central Gulf Coast: "If no fortress is placed at the Bay of Espíritu Santo and up to 500 men are not sent, the French will be able to take New Spain!"[6] In response, Spain ordered a mission and fort built close to the ruins of La Salle's old Fort St. Louis.

SAN ANTONIO. Roads were needed to carry supplies to the outlying settlements. De León's old route to northeast Texas served as the major pathway. The viceroy of New Spain decided to establish a post midway between the Rio Grande and the missions situated near the French danger. Captain Domingo Ramón identified a promising spot near San Pedro Springs: "There is sufficient water here for a city of more than one quarter league. The San Antonio River has a lovely pleasantness, for there are walnut trees, grapevines, willows, elms, and other timbers."[7]

In 1718 the first soldiers arrived and built Presidio of San Antonio de Béxar. Franciscans in their company founded Mission San Antonio de Valero (the Alamo). Two years later a priest traveled from East Texas to establish Mission San José. Inhabitants set about digging irrigation canals and raising corn, beans, and cotton.

Most of the soldiers at San Antonio were mestizos from the mining and ranching frontiers of northern Mexico. Lacking land at home, they welcomed the prospect of occupying their own tract in Texas. Some came with wives, intending to remain in the area when their tour of duty ended. A small village grew up around the fort.

But Spanish officials wanted a larger civilian presence. The difficulty lay in convincing families to become settlers. People living in

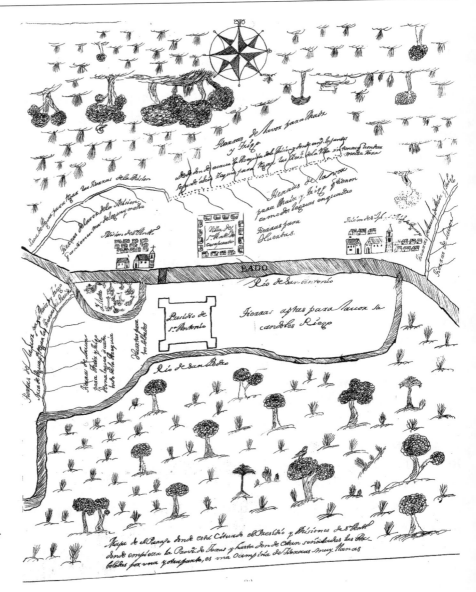

Map of San Antonio de Béxar Presidio and missions along the river, drawn by the Marqués de Aguayo, 1730. Institute of Texan Cultures illustration no. 68-2093

the cities of central Mexico, amid the comforts of civilization, showed no desire to move north to the wilderness of Texas. Recruiters turned to the Canary Islands, a territory off the western coast of Spain that was suffering from a drought. A small group of men, women, and children agreed to come. They sailed first to Veracruz and journeyed by land through Mexico to Texas.

In 1731 fifteen Canary Islander families, including two widows with children, arrived at San Antonio. Near the fort, the immigrants laid out the civilian town of San Fernando de Béxar and set about erecting homes and a church. To encourage them to come, Spain had offered the Canary Islanders control of the town government as well as title to lands that the original soldier-settlers had farmed and irrigated. Not surprisingly, the soldiers felt resentment. Tempers flared. A missionary railed against the new elite: "It is evident that the Islanders do not fit in this vast province. Here there is more unoccupied land than in all of Spain, but it all seems to them too small. They are so ambitious that they want everything for themselves. To this day there has never been such a people!"[8]

For their part, the Canary Islanders portrayed themselves as underprivileged. In a petition, they sought public pasture for their animals: "As you and the governor are well aware, we are but poor wretches barely able to support ourselves, having only our labor to sustain us. If we were to invest the time needed to watch and preserve our small horse herd, we would be placed now and in the long run in the most ruinous state imaginable!"[9]

Despite initial jealousy, relations among the groups mended with the passage of time. Isolation forced inhabitants of San Antonio to work together. Intermarriage and the tradition of godparenting among the settlers forged alliances. By 1800 the fort and town had merged into a single community known as Béxar.

MORE MISSIONS AND TOWNS. The network of Spanish settlements shifted several times during the eighteenth century, with missions opening, closing, and relocating. The missions of northeast Texas, newly established in 1716–17, were abandoned two years later following a skirmish with the French. They reopened in 1721, but within ten years three of these missions moved to San Antonio. The final three closed permanently in 1773. The mission on the bay near Fort St. Louis, Mission Espíritu Santo, was moved farther inland twice, the second time close to present-day Goliad.

▼▼▼

A presidio soldier courts a Canary Islands woman outside Mission San Antonio de Valero (the Alamo), mid–eighteenth century. Pen-and-ink drawing by José Cisneros, 1988. Institute of Texan Cultures illustration no. 88-374

The San Sabá Mission, which extended into Apache and Comanche territories, suffered disastrous consequences: in 1758 Indians attacked and burned the buildings, killing two priests along with several other people. José de Escandón, the midcentury colonizer, founded twenty-three towns in quick succession on both sides of the Rio Grande. Many of these towns had a mission nearby but lacked a fort to ward off attack. The size of the civilian community was considered sufficient protection.

Some of these new arrangements came about in response to changing defense needs and budget constraints. Spain and France were not *always* at war. At the close of the Seven Years' War, France transferred Louisiana to Spain. In 1768 the Marqués de Rubí completed an inspection tour of the Spanish borderlands. He concluded that it was no longer necessary to station troops at the Louisiana border. Instead, Spain should withdraw from East Texas and concentrate its defenses south of the Rio Grande. Rubí's report led to the final abandonment of the East Texas missions, as well as Los Adaes, a town in present-day Louisiana that had served as the capital of Spanish Texas.

One Los Adaes native, Antonio Gil Ibarbo, petitioned for permission to lead a group of settlers back to their homes closer to the Louisiana border. With the viceroy's approval, Ibarbo's group returned to the eastern woods, where they built the town of Bucareli. When Indian raids put that outpost in danger, they moved on to establish the town of Nacogdoches.

Some decisions stemmed from events in Europe and imperial strategies. Others came about almost by accident, by the whim or the forceful personality of a missionary, a government official, or a military commander. Authorities were often at odds with one another.

Amid these changes in the political landscape, residents of Spanish Texas established homes and went on with their daily lives. In the frontier region, they were creating a new identity, one distinct from the identity of people in the interior of Mexico.

MAKING A LIVING

SOLDIERS. The most reliable employer in the territories was typically the local fort. Recruits came from northern Mexico, pushed out by declining resources in minerals and land. These men raised on the frontier readily adapted to the rugged conditions and harsh demands they encountered in the north. Soldiers were issued ar-

Disappointed settlers abandon Los Adaes, 1773. Drawing by Sister M. Marietta. Institute of Texan Cultures illustration no. 71-39

mor made of quilted leather. They were responsible for keeping their own weapons in good repair. Troops suffered shortages of ammunition and other supplies as well as long delays in receiving their wages. Part of their military pay came in the form of food and other supplies. Procurement officers were not above withholding supplies or requiring enlisted men to buy shoddy goods at high prices.

Military service included defending settlers and repelling attacks by *los indios bárbaros*—Indians outside Spanish control. The troops were responsible for tracking down the Indians who escaped from the missions. A soldier who completed a ten-year enlistment would qualify for retirement benefits that included a plot of land. If he died, his wife received a widow's pension. Despite the uncertainties and hardships, volunteers enrolled in military service as a means of supporting their families.

FARMERS AND RANCHERS. When they arrived in Texas, the new settlers planted the seeds they brought from Mexico: maize, beans, peppers, melons, squash, and sugarcane. Land provided status to the owners. More important, farmland insured food for survival. When disputes arose, settlers went to court to defend their land claims and water rights.

In the South Texas brush, ranching ultimately proved more profitable than farming. Thousands of cattle roamed freely, descended from animals brought by early explorers. In the 1770s enterprising settlers began rounding up wild cattle, branding them, and driving them to markets in Louisiana and Mexico—the first Texas trail drives. Exports and uncontrolled killing greatly reduced the wild herds. In 1778 the Spanish government stepped in, declaring itself the owner of all unbranded cattle. The Texas governor offered a reward to citizens willing to turn in lawbreakers: "Anyone who denounces those whom he sees killing cattle, be they wild animals or of known ownership, shall receive the meat and tallow and one-half of the fine."[10]

ARTISANS AND MERCHANTS. Ranching and farming were the principal occupations in Spanish Texas. Persons who owned land in the countryside often maintained a residence in town. This provided a safe refuge in times of Indian attack.

Late-arriving immigrants might find the good farmlands already claimed. However, craftsmen with needed skills easily obtained work in the towns. Blacksmiths were warmly welcomed, for they could forge and repair tools, weapons, and other critical items. Teamsters hauled goods with oxcarts. Artisans made and sold pottery. Men hired themselves out as farmhands, carpenters, and stonemasons.

A few merchants opened stores. Because Spanish coins were in short supply, stores extended credit to customers. Barter served as the principal means of exchange. A surprising number of luxury goods made their way through Mexico to Texas, including porcelain dishes and silks shipped from the Orient.

Exchanging goods near San Fernando Church, San Antonio, mid–eighteenth century. Pen-and-ink drawing by José Cisneros, 1988. Institute of Texan Cultures illustration no. 88-377

▼▼▼

SPANISH MISSIONS

The Spanish colonial government intended the missions to be self-sufficient communities. European and Mexican-born missionaries traveled to the hinterlands to bring Catholic religion to the Indians. They provided training in the "virtues" of civilization—farming, animal husbandry, Spanish language, weaving, and other crafts, as well as religious instruction.

Within the mission, friars organized a strict schedule of prayer and work. Mission farmlands were held in communal ownership. Indian men learned to plant and harvest crops. Young children struggled to master spinning, while women performed cooking, laundering, and other domestic tasks.

While teaching Christianity and the skills needed for daily living in the Spanish style, friars tried to keep the Indians isolated inside the mission. The friars viewed soldiers, travelers, and traders as negative influences that could threaten the stability of mission life. "The missionary must not permit residents of the presidio or of another mission to play these games [of chance] with the Indians, because they are so taken up with the game, they would forfeit their blankets, their clothing and whatever they may have."[11]

Indians entered missions for protection, security, and the assurance of food. Once inside, they were likely to find their traditions challenged and discredited. Individual Indians found ways to resist, even while missionaries submitted glowing reports to their superiors. Some friars were honest enough to note the discontent they faced: "It seemed to me a good thing not to impose now any obligation to attend Mass, since it did not please them greatly to do so. ... When the bell is rung, some jump over the wall and some stay in their houses."[12]

Indians came to the missions from a variety of cultural backgrounds. Village Indians from the northeast, accustomed to raising their own food, refused to live within the walls of a mission. They resolutely continued to barter with French traders. In other places, Indians congregated when the missionary distributed provisions,

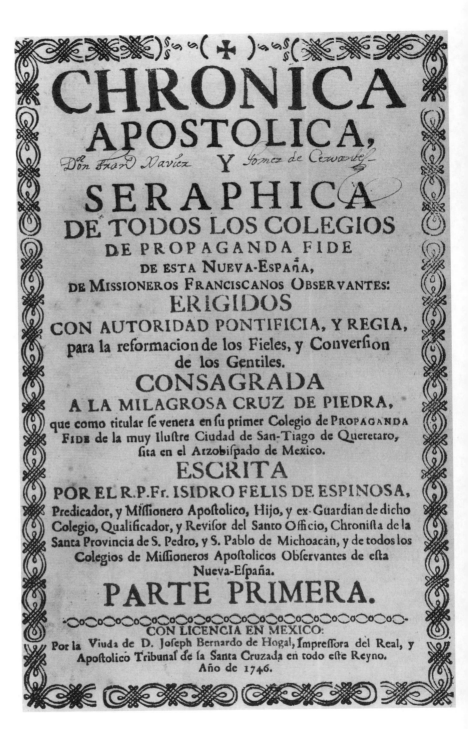

CHRONICA APOSTOLICA, Y SERAPHICA DE TODOS LOS COLEGIOS DE PROPAGANDA FIDE DE ESTA NUEVA-España, DE MISSIONEROS FRANCISCANOS OBSERVANTES: ERIGIDOS CON AUTORIDAD PONTIFICIA, Y REGIA, para la reformacion de los Fieles, y Conversion de los Gentiles. CONSAGRADA A LA MILAGROSA CRUZ DE PIEDRA, que como titular se venera en su primer Colegio de PROPAGANDA FIDE de la muy Ilustre Ciudad de San-Tiago de Queretaro, sita en el Arzobispado de Mexico. ESCRITA POR EL R.P.Fr. ISIDRO FELIS DE ESPINOSA, Predicador, y Missionero Apostolico, Hijo, y ex-Guardian de dicho Colegio, Qualificador, y Revisor del Santo Officio, Chronista de la Santa Provincia de S. Pedro, y S. Pablo de Michoacàn, y de todos los Colegios de Missioneros Apostolicos Observantes de esta Nueva-España. PARTE PRIMERA. CON LICENCIA EN MEXICO: Por la Viuda de D. Joseph Bernardo de Hogal, Impressora del Real, y Apostolico Tribunal de la Santa Cruzada en todo este Reyno. Año de 1746.

Title page to Chrónica Apostólica y Seráphica, *which listed instructions to Franciscan missionaries, 1746.* Institute of Texan Cultures illustration no. 68-2039

▼▼▼

26

then vanished when the season for hunting and gathering arrived. Indians in the Rio Grande Valley, unhindered by Spanish troops, traveled at will between the mission and town. Some worked as laborers for townspeople. Many intermarried and became absorbed into the town community. Missionaries adjusted certain rules to fit the local situation.

Missions along the San Antonio River came closest to fulfilling the Franciscan ideal of a self-contained, self-supporting compound. Indians in this area were subsistence hunter-gatherers with little military strength. They valued a secure food supply and protection from the marauding Plains tribes. Mission San José in San Antonio took in large numbers of new converts and grew to be the most prosperous mission in Texas. Downstream at Espíritu Santo, mission Indians herded and grazed thousands of cattle.

To attract and retain converts, friars distributed desired goods from the interior of Mexico: iron tools, beads, ribbons, and bolts of cloth. On special occasions they provided food and festivities within the walls of the compound, establishing traditions that can still be glimpsed in South Texas today: "On Christmas Eve there are prepared a kettle of beans, another of sweet potatoes, which if they are not planted at the mission, can be bought at the presidio. Regularly *buñuelos* [fried pastries] are made together with sweets which are then distributed. . . . The Indians do the dance of the *matachines* [religious reenactments] and go on dancing at the entrance of the friary as long as the missionary allows it. He generally gives them a drink if there is enough on hand."[13]

Indians living in the missions adopted some aspects of Catholicism and merged Christianity with their native religion. Nonetheless, they continued to gather in secret for traditional rituals. "Whenever the priests are not paying attention, the Indian men and women slip away to the woods to their *mitotes* [traditional native ritual] and dance with the pagan Indians. This practice is very much guarded against, and those who are caught are severely punished."[14]

For missionaries of an authoritarian outlook, these dance ceremonies posed a grave challenge. Other missionaries adopted a more

Mitote, ò baile de los Yndios Cumanches, y Apaches.

A European perspective on an Indian mitote, *appearing in Fray Juan Agustín Morfi's* History of Texas, *1779*. Institute of Texan Cultures illustration no. 68-2870

tolerant attitude, even noting parallels to habits of the Spanish. "Regarding the lawfulness of the dance called the *mitote* done by the Indians, whatever one can say about it, this much is certain: though some consider it evil the missionary does make allowances. The claim is that the Indians cling to their superstitious practices, and that for them this dance is like the fandango and *faraon* among the Spaniards."[15]

END OF THE MISSION ERA. Over time, Texas missions experienced a disturbing lack of residents. Several factors contributed to this decline. Some Indians slipped away when the Spanish failed to protect them from Apache or Comanche raids. Military commanders might refuse to pursue runaways and return them. Some of the fugitives preferred their earlier lifestyles. Others became truly adjusted to their new lives, moving into town and practicing trades. Spanish and mestizo settlers frequently married or formed unions with Indians, acquired Indian servants, or adopted Indian children. Finally, dreaded and recurrent epidemics swept through Texas further reducing the number of mission residents. Although these illnesses also affected the Spanish population, the native inhabitants were always more vulnerable to European diseases.

Ultimately, not enough Indians remained in missions to do the daily chores and tend the crops. As Texas missions continued to drain funds from the Treasury, the Spanish government decided to secularize them. Secularization meant removing missionaries from their post, assigning land titles to individual Indians, and distributing the remaining lands to other settlers. In the future, diocesan priests, not missionaries, would handle the religious needs of the populace.

Friars, unwilling to accept defeat, vigorously opposed these plans. They blamed the low morale at the missions on the indifference or neglect of government appointees: "We find ourselves at such an unfortunate time, when the gentlemen leaders consider that which is first as secondary and make the means an end. The least of their cares is the spiritual and temporal well-being of the missions and whether the gentiles are converted or not. It makes no difference to them if all the gentiles are condemned, since they do not believe in hell!"[16]

Protests went unheeded. One official penned his impressions to the viceroy: "They are a rendezvous of idlers and a haven for gamblers rather than true missions."[17] Weary of delays, the Texas governor ordered immediate secularization and turned over leadership of the missions to the local government officials. By the early 1800s, a number of missions were not simply secularized or unsupported but in ruins.

Most of what is known about individual women in the Spanish era comes from legal documents. In an age when few knew how to write, women did not keep diaries or personal histories of their own. Court records provide a glimpse into their lives and the standards of their society.

In 1735 a servant woman, Antonia Luzgarda Hernández, sued her former employer to regain custody of her son. Antonia was a free mulata *living in Texas. The word* mulata *refers to a person with one African parent and one Spanish parent. Unable to write, Antonia stated her case before a scribe: "While working in the house of Don Miguel Nuñez Morillo, I suffered such lack of decent clothing and mistreatment of my*

BUILDING A COMMUNITY

Settlers in Spanish Texas lived far from the seats of power in Mexico City and Seville. They tried to maintain Spanish customs and laws, but frontier conditions required adaptation and flexibility. Safety from Indian attack was an overriding concern. Settlers also worried about avoiding disease, acquiring needed tools, securing access to water, and saving sufficient food supplies to last during the lean times.

Faraway bureaucrats made decisions with little understanding of local conditions. For instance, in 1778 the Spanish government decided on a new Indian policy. Colonists were ordered to build alliances with the Comanche and, at the same time, to combat and isolate the Apache. This upset delicate balances of power and personal relationships that settlers had negotiated locally.

Spanish officials also tried to control ranching practices considered dangerous or vainglorious. They banned the hocking knife, a curved blade at the end of a long pole used to cripple animals for butchering. Frontier settlers ignored the ban; sometimes quarreling stockmen used hocking knives upon one another. Crown officials forbade the use of heavy iron cruciform stirrups, a fashion so unwieldy that a rider needed assistance mounting his horse. Yet ranchers in the distant borderlands continued to ride with them.

Throughout the eighteenth century, Spain strictly regulated trade in Texas, particularly with Louisiana and the French. The king of Spain rejected special requests that came from local officials: "Commerce with the French is not to be permitted under any circumstances, not even in wines and liquor, notwithstanding the harshness of that country and the scarcity of such that is experienced, and even though the Governor proposed it."[18]

Despite such proclamations, smugglers boldly exchanged contraband goods. Louisiana had long been—and remained—Texas' natural trading partner.

Texas towns with roots in the colonial period included San Antonio, Goliad, and Nacogdoches. Laredo, mapped inside another province during the colonial era, became part of Texas in the nineteenth century as did the western Rio Grande villages of Ysleta, Socorro, and San Elizario. San Antonio de Béxar was easily the largest town in Spanish Texas and the only one to have its own town council.

The town council of San Antonio tried mightily to regulate local affairs. It organized public celebrations on feast days of the Virgin of Guadalupe, the Virgin of Candlemas, and other saints. Leading citizens sponsored these events, paying the bills for bullfights, processions, ceremonies, and festive foods. When activities got out of hand, the Texas governor stepped in to impose order:

> Inasmuch as today is the feast of St. John, and since also on feasts of St. Peter, St. James, and St. Ann, citizens, including women, traditionally celebrate by holding parades on horseback up and down the town's streets; and because these outings often turn into horse races, creating dangerous situations, and causing a variety of accidents and mishaps; and because I see it as my duty to protect the citizenry from danger, I command the following: All citizens, regardless of class, social status or profession, who wish to indulge in horse racing must refrain from doing so in the streets of the town and of its presidio. . . . Violators . . . will be sentenced to one month in jail, doing hard labor on the government building project, in shackles, and without pay or sustenance.
>
> *Domingo Cabello*
> *Governor of Texas, 1781*[19]

WOMEN. Women in Spanish colonies lived in a society dominated by men. The church set standards of acceptable behavior, demanding stricter standards for women than for men. Few girls received instruction in reading or writing. Despite such constraints, Spanish colonial women raised orphans and adopted Indian children. They cooked and healed with resources available from the land. They took part in social festivities, including, apparently, the reckless horse races that so disturbed the governor. A young woman might find herself

humble person that I left . . . taking two children with me, one of whom I brought when I entered the house of Don Miguel, and one to whom I gave birth in his home. For no other reason than this, that his wife had baptized the said infant, he, exercising absolute power, snatched away from me the only man I have, who I hope in time will support me."

Don Miguel protested that a "spiritual relationship" linked his wife to Antonia's son. Since his birth, she had been his godmother. Despite Don Miguel's argument, the magistrate returned the boy to his mother.

In 1782 Francisca Martínez brought a land claim against another woman. To strengthen her case, she pointed out the military record and reputation of her family. "It seems

31

to me that I have more right to the land than Margarita Ximénez, because I bought it from the recognized owner, have lived on it sixteen years, and because I am a poor widow. My husband as well as my father died in the service of His Majesty."

The court found in Francisca's favor. It noted that not only was she a military wife but a widow who had conducted herself in an exemplary manner. "She has raised his children well, and has constructed a stone house on the lot." An official arranged the formal ceremony of occupation. "I took Francisca Martínez by the hand, led her to the place, and walked over it with her. She threw stones, shouted, and made other demonstrations of true and lawful possession."

Women of Spanish Texas. Pen-and-ink drawings by José Cisneros. Institute of Texan Cultures illustration nos. 88-369

wooed by soldiers from the local fort. For a soldier, marrying the daughter of a prominent family could increase his prestige in the community.

Spanish colonial women actually had more legal rights than most women of the world in their time. A daughter inherited equally with her brothers. A bride remained the owner of any possessions that were hers at the time of the marriage. Property acquired *during* a marriage belonged equally to both partners. This law is the origin of the community property law that still operates in Texas today.

The father of an unmarried daughter managed her property and made financial decisions on her behalf. For a married woman, her husband exercised this authority, but he could not sell his wife's property without her consent. Widows gained the legal standing of a man. They could enter into contracts, buy and sell land, and conduct business transactions. In the 1824 census, women who claimed to be widows headed 30 percent of San Antonio's households.[20]

Sources: Petition of Antonia Luzgarda Hernández to Governor Manuel de Sandoval, Aug. 9, 1735, Bexar Archives, Center for American History, University of Texas at Austin, translation from Bexar Archives Translations, Center for American History, Austin; Litigation between Francisca Martínez and Margarita Ximénes over ownership of property, June, 1782, Bexar County Spanish Archives, Book Misc-2, Bexar County Courthouse, San Antonio, trans. Dora Elizondo Guerra.

A baptism in San Fernando Church, San Antonio, 1740. Pen-and-ink drawing by José Cisneros. Institute of Texan Cultures illustration no. 88-370

A Spanish Texas woman with a grievance could bring her case to court, even if she came from a poor family or was unable to sign her petition. Women seem to have been quite aware of this option. Colonial archives contain records of women who contested land ownership, land boundaries, pensions, broken contracts, domestic mistreatment, and child custody.

SOCIAL CLASS. Class distinctions existed in the Texas frontier as they did throughout New Spain. Owning land brought status. Community leaders and men who held title to large tracts of land were addressed with the honorary title "Don." Special prestige came to residents who could trace their descent from the original founders.

A latecomer who missed the original distribution of lands might still rise in social rank. He could marry a daughter or widow of a long-established family. If he had a manual skill like carpentry or stonework, he could earn enough money to purchase land. Family alliances were forged when godparents pledged responsibility for a baby.

Some freed slaves found their way to Texas frontier settlements, as did *castas,* people of mixed Old World–New World ancestry. Immigrants labeled as castas typically took jobs of low status like servant or day laborer.

Spain had developed an elaborate system of labeling people according to their bloodlines. The child of a Spaniard and an Indian was a *mestizo;* the child of a mestizo and an Indian was a *coyote,* and so on for various possible combinations. Race for each person was noted on the census listing. Although this system operated fairly rigidly in the Mexican interior, on the frontier the categories appear to have been negotiable. People who married well or acquired property might change their racial classification from one census to the next.

The category of highest status was *español,* pure Spaniard. By the 1793 census, 74 percent of San Antonio's residents were listed as "Spanish."[21] This census seems very doubtful as an objective measure of ancestry. Immigrants to Texas came mainly from northern

Mexico, where people had mingled and intermarried for over two centuries.

In colonial Texas, the term "Spaniard" seems to have been more a social category than a racial one. Most settlers could reasonably aspire to higher status through land ownership, marriage, and wealth.

▼▼▼

CHAPTER 2

Weathering a Century of Change, 1800–1900

$\mathcal{A}$T THE START OF the nineteenth century, perhaps five thousand colonial settlers lived in Texas, half of them at San Antonio de Béxar. Despite repeated efforts, Spain had been unable to fill Texas with enough people to ward off Indian attacks or prevent meddling by foreigners. For settlers, frontier scarcities and distance built self-reliance. This hardy and sometimes cocky population resented Spain's efforts to tighten controls in the late 1700s, when the Crown issued regulations raising taxes, asserting ownership of wild cattle, requiring citizens to participate in building projects, and forbidding Louisiana trade.

Despite local rumblings, Texas remained a backwater and minor irritant for Spanish administrators. Then an uprising in Mexico set in motion a chain of events that brought settlers from the United States into Texas and changed its social fabric forever.

THE FADING OF THE SPANISH EMPIRE

REVOLT IN MEXICO, 1810. The class system in Mexico operated more oppressively than it did in Texas. Many people in Mexico felt little hope of improving their lives. Spaniards from Spain, *peninsulares,* controlled most of the wealth and power. Below them functioned a lesser elite of *criollos,* individuals born in America to

Miguel Hidalgo y Costilla, 1753–1811, leader of Mexican independence. Hidalgo's supporters carried a banner of the Virgin of Guadalupe into battle. Institute of Texan Cultures illustration no. 76-178

Spanish parents. Below them were *peones,* people of mixed races who comprised the majority population and worked in the menial jobs. Lowest of all were the remaining indigenous peoples, who faced conditions of sickness, exploitation, and poverty.

The conditions of the people were ripe for an independence

movement. In the late eighteenth century, the European Enlightenment had excited intellectuals with ideas of freedom and natural rights. People of the Spanish colonies could draw inspiration from the examples of the recent American and French Revolutions. Spain was preoccupied by difficulties in Europe, culminating in 1808 when the French emperor Napoleon invaded Spain and placed his brother on its throne.

In central Mexico, Miguel Hidalgo y Costilla, a *criollo* priest, issued a public call for independence from Spain. The date of his *grito,* or cry, was September 16, 1810. It would become a national holiday in Mexico.

People from various social classes flocked to his cause. The rebels won several skirmishes before losing a major battle. Father Hidalgo was headed to Texas in search of help when he was captured, put on trial, and executed. The independence movement did not end, however. In the far corners of New Spain, including Texas, people used the opportunity to encourage local uprisings against the government.

REVOLT IN TEXAS, 1811–13. In January, 1811, a retired presidio officer living in San Antonio declared the rebels against Spain, rallied local troops, and removed the Spanish governor. Within weeks, however, reports reached Texas that the rebel armies were faltering in Mexico. Worried ranchers and several elite families in San Antonio mounted a counterrevolution, ousting the army officer and restoring royal officials.

Soon another revolutionary army appeared, this time bringing foreigners to Texas. José Bernardo Gutiérrez de Lara, a native of northern Mexico, had negotiated with Americans in Washington, D.C., and Louisiana, which was now part of the United States. Gutiérrez and his new American associates raised recruits for what they called the Republican Army of the North. The word "republic" meant a nation without a king. By including it in their name, the group was declaring their opposition to the Spanish Crown. They entered Texas through Louisiana, seized control of Nacogdoches, and then moved into the fort at La Bahía.

The Texas governor besieged them there, but he was unable to keep reinforcements from reaching them. When he withdrew the siege, the rebel forces defeated the government troops. In spring, 1813, Gutiérrez and his Republican Army of the North marched triumphantly into San Antonio.

Gutiérrez enjoyed the support of several leading families in the region, but local support wavered when he brutally murdered the governor and other captives. Gutiérrez quarreled with his American cohorts over control. He wrote a constitution for Texas that favored the Spanish-speaking population.

Crown officials in Mexico sent a seasoned officer, Joaquín de Arredondo, to dislodge the intruders. Arredondo arrived in Texas at the head of a royal army. By then Gutiérrez had been banished by the rebels. The Mexican general defeated the occupying forces and undertook a campaign to arrest and kill suspected republican sympathizers.

Many longtime Texas residents felt compelled to flee for their lives. José Antonio Navarro and Erasmo Seguín escaped to Louisiana, where they found work as common laborers. José Francisco Ruiz sought refuge with Indians. Some settlers' property was confiscated. Texas remained firmly in royalist hands until 1821, when Mexico succeeded in winning its independence from Spain.

LIFE IN MEXICAN TEXAS, 1821–36

With Mexico now an independent nation, residents of Texas were truly Mexican Texans. They had little doubt of their ability to live under the new government, which after all would continue their language, religion, and customs. But Texas had suffered devastation in the turmoil since 1810: half of its population had left, Indian raids increased in number, and many ranchers no longer dared to tend their livestock.

▼▼▼

ENCOURAGING SETTLEMENT. Mexico inherited Spain's problems of protecting and populating its northern frontier. As a solution, the Mexican government invited foreigners, which included people in the United States, to settle Texas. Stephen F. Austin received permission to bring three hundred Catholic families to Texas. Afterward, Mexico signed similar agreements with other *empresarios,* or land developers, allowing them to move in foreigners, issue land to them, and establish colonies. The immigrants pledged to practice the Catholic religion, obey Mexican law, and become Mexican citizens.

Spanish-speaking residents born in Texas—who were starting to call themselves *tejanos*—generally welcomed the newcomers. Elite families in particular saw opportunities for commercial partnerships and trade with the United States. Immigrants could plant cotton on the idle land, discourage Indian raids, and make the region safe for ranching. Population growth would boost the region's prosperity.

Settlers from the United States poured into Texas. Their numbers soon overwhelmed the native-born residents. By the early 1830s, there were roughly thirty thousand settlers from the United States and Europe, compared to about four thousand Tejanos.[1]

The land grant system fell into some difficulties. Along the coast and elsewhere, the Mexican government issued grants to immigrants for lands already inhabited by Tejanos. The new settlers made decisions in their own interests, disregarding the needs and desires of their Tejano neighbors. Tejanos of Goliad complained to their state legislature in 1833, "Let us be honest with ourselves, Sir, the foreign *empresarios* are nothing more than money-changing speculators caring only for their own well-being."[2]

A CHANGING SOCIETY. Even as new Anglo towns arose, San Antonio remained an important cultural center. Its residents, who were nearly all of Spanish descent, continued to hold their traditional fiestas. Church, military, and local officials joined together to plan activities for Catholic saints' days, Christmas, and the new Mexican

▼▼▼

Riders greet their dates for a dance. Oil painting by Theodore Gentilz, a French artist who visited San Antonio in the mid-1800s and painted scenes of everyday life. Institute of Texan Cultures illustration no. 72-653

Independence Day. Activities typically included booths, games, a dance, a religious mass, and a military salute. Since colonial times, these civic festivities had helped to build a sense of identity.

Yet travelers to Texas during this period found that society was changing due to the influence of Americans. Some visitors kept journals of their impressions. Jean Louis Berlandier, writing in 1828, observed: "Trade with the Anglo Americans, and the blending to some degree of their customs, make the inhabitants of Texas a little different from Mexicans of the interior. . . . In their gatherings, the women prefer to dress in the fashion of Louisiana, and by so doing they participate both in the customs of the neighboring nation and their own."[3] José María Sánchez, a Mexican army officer visiting Texas in the same year, noted changes as well. "The Mexicans who live here are a very humble people, and perhaps their intentions are good, but because of their education and environment they are ignorant not only of the customs of our great cities, but even of the occurrences of our Revolution. . . . Accustomed to the continued trade with the North Americans, they have adopted their customs and habits, and one may say truly they are not Mexicans except by birth, for they even speak Spanish with a marked incorrectness."[4]

STRUCTURING A NEW GOVERNMENT. In the interior of Mexico, meanwhile, politicians struggled over what type of government to adopt. Centralists wanted a strong central government with authority concentrated in Mexico City. Federalists wanted the individual states of Mexico to retain important powers, especially the authority to regulate local affairs. Inhabitants of Texas, who had a long tradition of championing their interests against distant authorities, tended to side with the federalists.

Mexican federalists wrote and produced the Constitution of 1824, one of the most liberal documents anywhere in the world at that time. This document set up a government that emphasized states' rights and civil rights.

DISSENT IN TEXAS. In 1829 the federalist president of Mexico, Vicente Guerrero, issued a proclamation freeing slaves in the Mexican republic. This emancipation law displeased Anglos living in Texas. Many had come from plantations in the U.S. South and brought slaves to do the work. Some native-born Tejanos joined Anglos in protesting this law. They won an exemption that allowed slavery to continue in Texas.

Soon afterward the centralists rose to power in Mexico. Alarmed by the huge number of Anglos in Texas—many of whom were trading illegally and ignoring other Mexican laws—the centralists passed the Law of April 6, 1830. This prohibited further immigration

▼▼▼

from the United States and further importation of slaves. It required customs duties on goods from the United States. Foreigners were barred from practicing retail trade in Texas.

Cries rose in protest. For a time federalists returned to power in Mexico, and it looked as if a compromise could be worked out with the unhappy Texans. Then in 1834, General Antonio López de Santa Anna gained control of the Mexican government. He disbanded the state legislatures and abolished the Constitution of 1824. This action pushed Anglo Texans to the breaking point. Santa Anna was opposed also by many Tejanos.

THE TEJANO DILEMMA. Mexican Texans were in a quandary. They had business and personal relationships with the Anglo immigrants. Some had married into their families. For example, young Ursula Veramendi, from one of San Antonio's most prominent families, was the wife of Jim Bowie.

Many Tejanos favored a restoration of the Constitution of 1824 but balked at a complete break with the mother country. Some sensed that under an independent Texas, they would lose status and protection as a minority population. However, events moved too swiftly to stop the tide of independence.

TEXAS WAR OF INDEPENDENCE, 1835–36

INITIAL MANEUVERS. Hostilities broke out when local settlers at Gonzales and Mexican troops quarreled over possession of a cannon. The Mexican commander withdrew. Shortly afterwards, Stephen F. Austin took command of the volunteers assembled at Gonzales and led them toward San Antonio, where the Mexican centralist army was encamped. Austin appointed Texas native Juan N. Seguín a captain and urged him to recruit a company of horsemen among the Tejano ranchers of the region. Seguín promptly did so. His unit kept Austin's troops supplied with corn, beans, beef, and other provisions from the countryside.

In December, 1835, Tejanos and Anglos united to storm San Antonio de Béxar. The Mexican commander, General Cos, surrendered and withdrew his troops south of the Rio Grande. Most Anglo volunteers then returned home, confident they had seen the last centralist army in Texas until spring—or possibly, forever. The small garrison that stayed behind needed food, and the townspeople obliged.

SIEGE OF THE ALAMO. Early in February, 1836, Juan Seguín's scouts reported that Santa Anna was leading a large army across the Rio Grande into Texas. Panic broke out in San Antonio. Caught in a revolution not of their making, most native Tejanos tried to stay out of harm's way. Families loaded carts and left to seek shelter with relatives who owned ranches in the countryside. J. M. Rodriguez, a child during the Texas Revolution, later recalled his

Built before 1780, the Veramendi House was probably the most elegant home in colonial San Antonio. The paneled doors opened into a high entrance hall, a patio, and a series of garden terraces leading down to the river. Photographed in the 1860s, demolished 1909. Institute of Texan Cultures illustration no. 81-500

▼▼▼

TEXAS!!

Emigrants who are desirious of assisting Texas at this important crisis of her affairs may have a free passage and equipments, by applying at the **NEW-YORK and PHILADELPHIA HOTEL,** On the Old Levee, near the Blue Stores.

Now is the time to ensure a fortune in Land: To all who remain in Texas during the War will be allowed 1280 Acres. To all who remain Six Months, 640 Acres. To all who remain Three Months, 320 Acres. And as Colonists, 4600 Acres for a family and 1470 Acres for a Single Man. New Orleans, April 23d, 1836.

Advertisement recruiting Americans to Texas during the independence movement, 1836. Institute of Texan Cultures illustration no. 68-422

family's hurried departure: "My father being away with General Houston's army, my mother undertook to act for us and decided it was best for us to go into the country to avoid being here when General Santa Anna's army should come in. We went to the ranch of Doña Santos Ximenes. We left in ox carts."[5] Eulalia Yorba, a resident of Béxar during the siege of the Alamo, felt similar dread. In 1896 she described her experience. "Of course I kept at home with my little boys and never stirred out once, for we women were all terribly frightened. Every eatable in the house, all the cows, lumber and hay about the place were taken by [Santa Anna's] troops, but we were assured that if we remained in the house no personal harm would come to us."[6]

Santa Anna entered San Antonio with two thousand troops on February 23, 1836. The Texian forces that remained in town barricaded themselves inside the Alamo, an old mission in ruins, under the command of young William Barret Travis.

At least nine native Tejanos joined the Alamo defenders and died with them on March 6. Juan Seguín was originally part of the Alamo contingent, but Travis dispatched him to Goliad on February 28 carrying a desperate plea for reinforcements—a plea that went unanswered. Several of the Mexican Texans brought their wives and children with them into the fort. When the Alamo fell, Santa Anna's soldiers did not kill the women and children but took them to the general as ordered. Santa Anna interviewed the noncombatants, gave each family a blanket and some coins, and sent them away.

BREAK WITH THE MOTHERLAND. Most Tejanos involved in the hostilities believed they were fighting to restore constitutional government in Mexico. But during the Alamo siege, a convention of delegates met at Washington-on-the-Brazos and decided to pursue a complete break with Mexico. Three men of Mexican descent, José Francisco Ruiz, José Antonio Navarro, and Lorenzo de Zavala, were among the fifty-nine signers of the Texas Declaration of Independence. Ruiz and his nephew Navarro belonged to a prominent San Antonio family that had long supported U.S. immigration. Lorenzo de Zavala was a liberal politician from the Yucatán in Mexico. He had come to Texas to promote his land contracts and to escape Santa Anna's displeasure.

In the East Texas town of Nacogdoches, Tejanos tried to sit out the revolt. Pressured by a military draft, they formed a militia unit under Vicente Córdova. Córdova struck an agreement with the local commander that the Tejanos would be responsible for defending Nacogdoches against Indians and local raiders, but they would not take up arms against their Mexican countrymen.

After the Alamo battle, Juan Seguín gathered his forces at Gonzales with Sam Houston, commander of the main Texas force. When news of the Declaration of Independence arrived, Seguín's men were asked to swear allegiance to an independent Texas, and they did so. These troops fought alongside General Houston at the

In 1836 Enrique Esparza was an eight-year-old living with his family in San Antonio de Béxar. The town buzzed with rumors that Santa Anna was bringing a large army to take revenge. Enrique's father, who was in the Texas forces, tried to arrange for his wife and children to leave town, but the army arrived too quickly. The family took refuge inside the Alamo. Although his father died defending the fort, Enrique and the other family members survived.

Many years later, Enrique described their experience. "There were six of us besides my father: my mother, whose name was Anita; my elder sister, myself, and three younger brothers, one a baby in arms. . . . It took a whole day to move, and an hour before sundown we were in the fort. There

The Esparza family seeking refuge inside the Alamo, February, 1836. Drawing by Thom Ricks. Institute of Texan Cultures illustration no. 82-31

Battle of San Jacinto. The Tejanos took the precaution of identifying themselves, because anti-Mexican sentiment was running high after the deaths at the Alamo and Goliad. One officer recalled, "During the Battle of San Jacinto, the battle cry of the Texans was 'Remember the Alamo,' and they made me take my men who were Mexicans and put large pieces of white pasteboard on their hats and breasts, lest they should be mistaken for Santa Anna's men and killed."[7]

The Battle of San Jacinto ended with the defeat of the Mexican army and the capture of Santa Anna. As a condition of his release, Santa Anna signed a treaty recognizing the independence of Texas. The Mexican government rejected this treaty, claiming that Santa Anna had no authority to sign it. But Mexico was unable to retake Texas, so independence became an established fact. The Texans proceeded to set up a government and conduct the affairs of a nation state.

LIFE IN THE TEXAS REPUBLIC, 1836—45

POLITICAL REALIGNMENT. Under independent Texas, citizens of Mexican descent lost political influence. The new government was patterned after the American system. Anglos held most elective positions. Only four Tejanos served in the new Republic of Texas congress: Seguín, Ruiz, Navarro, and Rafael Calixto de la Garza. These four men proposed bills to benefit their native constituents—especially regarding land and language issues—but many of their bills failed to pass. At the state constitutional convention of 1845, Navarro almost single-handedly defeated an attempt to deny the vote to Mexicans in Texas.[8]

Significantly, all of the Tejanos in the congress were from San Antonio de Béxar, which remained a stronghold of Mexican influence. Visitors to San Antonio noted its unique cultural flavor as something quite different from the atmosphere in newer Anglo settlements. William Bollaert, a British visitor in 1843, reported: "The Maromeros, or Mexican rope dancers are jumping about this evening. Although San Antonio is governed by Texan laws, Mexican customs prevail: rope dancing, tumbling, and plays on a Sunday!"[9]

Locally in San Antonio, Tejanos held a majority of city council seats. Council minutes were recorded in both English and Spanish. However, only once during this period was San Antonio's mayor of Mexican descent. Several of the Anglo mayors, as well as lesser officials, had wooed their wives from among the Tejano community. San Antonio's old families and the new Anglo elite joined together to attend social events. In 1838 Mary Maverick, wife of Anglo mayor Samuel Maverick, noted, "our only society are Mexicans."[10]

Religious presence in Texas also changed. Catholicism, no longer the state religion, lost its predominance. Most of the incoming Anglos were Protestant. Protestant missionaries gained some Mexican converts. The Catholic Church placed Texas under the ecclesiastical jurisdiction of New Orleans and sent a Frenchman, Jean Marie Odin, to head the church in Texas. Odin removed two native-born Tejano priests and made other changes when he arrived in San Antonio.

was a bridge over the river about where Commerce Street crosses it, and just as we got to it, we could hear Santa Anna's drums beating on Milam Square."

During the thirteen-day siege, Enrique stayed with his siblings and mother in a small room off the Alamo chapel. When the fighting ended, Mexican soldiers found the women and children huddled in a corner of the little room. At dawn, guards led them past the bodies and out of the fort. One by one the women went before Santa Anna to be interviewed. When his mother Anita was called, Enrique kept a nervous watch. "My brother was clinging to her skirt, but I stood to one side and behind her. I watched every move and listened to every word."

From questioning Anita, Santa Anna learned that the family

▼▼▼

had other relatives in San Antonio. He told her she was free to go. Enrique's uncle, Francisco Esparza, had fought on the Mexican side with Santa Anna's forces. Francisco received permission to search for his brother's body among the dead. He recovered the body and buried it in the city cemetery.

Enrique Esparza remained in Texas, farming in Atascosa and Bexar Counties and hauling goods between San Antonio and the Gulf Coast. After some delay, he received land as a surviving relative of an Alamo defender.

Sources: Enrique Esparza, interview in *San Antonio Express,* Nov. 22, 1902, reprinted in Timothy M. Matovina, *The Alamo Remembered: Tejano Accounts and Perspectives* (Austin: University of Texas Press, 1995), pp. 68–72; Enrique Esparza, interview in *San Antonio Express,* May 19, 1907, reprinted in Matovina, *Alamo Remembered,* pp. 78–89; Crystal Sasse Ragsdale, *The Women and Children of the Alamo* (Austin: The State House Press, 1994), pp. 79–87.

Juan Neponuceno Seguín

Tejano revolutionists. Pen-and-ink drawings by José Cisneros, based on life portraits. Institute of Texan Cultures illustration no. 88-369

▼▼▼

CITIZEN SUSPECTS. In the new Texas nation, people of Mexican descent were being accused of treason and collaboration with Mexico. Some families who had fled during the turmoil tried to return but found their lands occupied. Anglo immigrants challenged Tejano land claims and declared their lands forfeit. In a letter to a colleague, Bishop Jean Marie Odin reported the injustices he had seen: "The volunteers coming from the United States to help Texas and several Texan individuals to whom the protection of the frontier was entrusted do not cease to commit the most shameful depredations; they steal from the poor inhabitants of the valley of San Antonio all that they possess: corn, animals, nothing is spared. Entire villages have been devastated. Several families have had to abandon the land in order to escape the violence of every kind."[11]

From the Alamo, William Barret Travis himself had denounced Tejanos. During the siege, he penned a message demanding punishment for any residents who had not proven their allegiance: "The citizens of this municipality are all our enemies, except for those who have joined us heretofore. We have three Mexicans now at the fort; those who have not joined us in this extremity should be declared public enemies, and their property should aid in paying the expenses of the war."[12]

In actuality, Tejanos had fought on both sides of the military actions in Texas. Sometimes families were divided, as in the case of the Esparza family—Gregorio died defending the Alamo, while his brother Francisco served with Santa Anna's army. Some Tejanos switched sides during the course of events. They realized that the consequences of supporting a losing army could be severe. Many Tejanos professed neutrality and simply tried to avoid the fighting. Upon their return, they encountered hostility from their neighbors. A number of families, facing threats and discouragement, decided to move permanently to Mexico.

THE CÓRDOVA REVOLT. In East Texas, Vicente Córdova watched in frustration as Tejanos lost property and livelihood. In 1838 he led an uprising of dispossessed settlers who were mainly Tejanos but

Juan N. Seguín, Dishonored Patriot

Juan N. Seguín was born in 1806 to an old Texas family. His great-great-grandfather had been one of the original founders of San Antonio in the 1720s. Seguín played a role in practically every significant event in Mexican Texas and the Texas Revolution. Yet incredibly, he accompanied a Mexican army in 1842 to fight against Texas. The dilemmas that he faced—of loyalty, identity, and security—troubled other Mexican Texans in the nineteenth century.

Seguín's father was a local politician and a friend of Stephen F. Austin. Following in his father's footsteps, young Juan won his first elective office at the age of twenty-two. By 1834 he was alcalde *(mayor) and political chief of San Antonio.*

In the Texas Revolu-

included a few Anglos, Indians, and blacks. They issued a proclamation declaring their intent "to protect their individual rights and those of the Nation to which they belong."[13]

Córdova hoped for support from local Indian tribes and the Mexican government. Most of the promised aid never materialized. Government militias pursued Córdova's followers, isolating them and breaking their strength. Tejano citizens in Nacogdoches faced arrest, including those who had played no role in the uprising. Córdova escaped to Mexico.

Although some individual Indians had joined Córdova, no Indian nation committed itself to his cause. Nonetheless, the failed revolt was used to justify removing Cherokees and other native peoples from East Texas.[14]

MEXICAN ATTEMPTS TO RETAKE TEXAS. In South Texas, accusations against Tejanos peaked in 1842. Mexico, still chafing at its loss, twice invaded and occupied San Antonio that year. During the first invasion, Mayor Juan Seguín considered the size of the Mexican army and advised evacuating the city. For his efforts Seguín was labeled a traitor and a Mexican spy. Texas forces later recaptured San Antonio, but Seguín felt compelled to flee the young republic for his life.

CONSERVING IDENTITY. Tejanos faced a new reality as a minority population in a land they had settled. They sought to emphasize allegiance to Texas while preserving Mexican customs. As they had since colonial times, Tejanos formed alliances through intermarriage and godparenting, this time with the new Anglo immigrants.

Mexican Texan women continued to serve their traditional foods—corn tortillas, tamales, *frijoles* (beans), chiles, *cabrito* (kid goat), and *nopalitos* (cactus leaves). They prepared tortillas on a daily basis, first soaking corn in water that had been mixed with powdered lime. When the husks were soft, the women ground the corn on a stone metate, adding a few drops of the lime water to make a

Juan Nepomuceno Seguín, 1806–90. Institute of Texan Cultures illustration no. 68-470

masa paste. Finally the cooks took a pinch of the *masa,* patted it with their hands into a round shape, and heated it on a flat griddle over the fire.

Tejanos living on ranches displayed horsemanship skills that they had refined over generations. They continued to utilize the equipment and methods developed in the colonial period. When ranch work was slow, they made lariats and bridles by braiding rawhide or the soft hair from horses' manes. Many words spoken by Spanish stockmen have entered the English language including: *arroyo*/arroyo, *bronco*/bronco, *cañón*/canyon, *chaparral*/chaparral, *corral*/corral, *cuarta*/quirt, *estampida*/stampede, *la reata*/lariat, *lazo*/lasso, *mesteño*/mustang, *palomino*/palomino, *pinto*/pinto, *rancho*/ranch, *rodeo*/rodeo, and *vaquero*/buckaroo.

tion, Seguín raised a company of Tejano troops to assist Houston and Austin. During the siege of the Alamo, he joined the defenders in the fort. He escaped death only because Travis sent him on a fruitless mission to seek reinforcements. Seguín and his band joined with Anglos in defeating Santa Anna at the Battle of San Jacinto.

By 1837 Seguín was back in San Antonio. He gave the funeral oration when ashes of the Alamo defenders were moved and buried. Amid reports that the Mexican army was again on the move, Seguín received a stark order to abandon and burn San Antonio. Reluctant to destroy his native city, he appealed to Commander-in-Chief Sam Houston. Houston reconsidered and rescinded the order.

During the Texas Republic, Seguín served as senator from San

Antonio and garnered profits from land sales. Yet he was well aware of the plight of fellow Mexican Texans. "The straggling American adventurers were already beginning to work their dark intrigues against the native families, whose only crime was that they owned large tracts of land and desirable property."

In 1842, while Seguín was mayor, a Mexican army again arrived to take San Antonio. This time he did advise withdrawing from the town. Rumors spread that he was operating as a Mexican spy.

Receiving threats to his life, Seguín fled to Mexico, where he was immediately arrested and jailed. Mexican authorities offered to release him if he would join an army marching to reconquer Texas. Seguín, concerned for his wife and seven children, reluctantly agreed. "At

Fandango in San Antonio, painted ca. 1848 by Theodore Gentilz. Institute of Texan Cultures illustration no. 68-545

A favored form of entertainment was the *fandango,* a spirited community dance. Couples promenaded to music provided by guitars, fiddles, or violins. They partook of festive foods. Typically these gatherings included drinking and gambling. Anglo visitors attended out of curiosity. One man was shocked to see a fandango "in which the priest and all participated, so contrary to all my pre-conceived notions of propriety."[15] Bullfights, cockfights, and horse racing provided additional entertainment for the men.

Tejano leaders continued to hold the distinct religious and civic celebrations that had originated in colonial times. They welcomed outsiders to participate. Eyewitnesses described how San Antonio honored December 12, feast day of the Virgin of Guadalupe, during the early 1840s. First, women decorated the church and festively adorned an image of the Virgin of Guadalupe. Then the event began with a long procession of young girls wearing white who held candles and carried the image of the Virgin on a platform. Fiddlers walked alongside playing music. A military escort fired rifles and a cannon in salute. Participants then gathered inside the San Fernando Church for a religious service. Some parishioners later attended an all-night dance in a local home.[16]

Commemoration of Guadalupe extended back to the Spanish Conquest era. By continuing this ritual, Mexican Texans affirmed their heritage and identity. Today, as in earlier times, this commemoration honors indigenous people and women. Women known as *Guadalupanas* play a major role in preparing the feast-day event.

LIFE IN AMERICAN TEXAS, 1846–1900

NEW ALIGNMENTS AND WARS. Lured by land, hundreds of immigrants poured into Texas from the United States and Europe. The population of Texas tripled in the nine years following independence.

Procession for the feast day of the Virgin of Guadalupe, San Antonio, December, 1933. Institute of Texan Cultures illustration no. 0140-F

last the father triumphed over the citizen: I seized the sword that pained my hand."

He accompanied General Adrian Woll in the Mexican commander's campaign to retake Texas, but the attempt ended in failure. During the U.S.-Mexican War of 1846–48, Seguín fought on the side of Mexico.

Afterward Seguín returned to Texas and attempted to resume his old life. He won election to local offices and helped establish the Democratic Party in his county, but he faced severe criticism. Anxious to clear his name, he wrote a defense in 1858. It began with anguished words of betrayal: "A native of the city of San Antonio de Béxar, I embraced the cause of Texas at the sound of the first cannon which foretold her liberty. . . . In the very land which in other times bestowed on *me such bright and repeated evidences of trust and esteem, I now find myself . . . a foreigner in my native land."*

In his later years, Seguín sold his land in Texas and retired with his wife to Mexico. He died in Nuevo Laredo in 1890. Seguín, veteran of many decisive actions, remains a complex and ambivalent figure in Texas history.

Source: Jesús F. de la Teja, ed., *A Revolution Remembered: The Memoirs and Selected Correspondence of Juan N. Seguín* (Austin: State House Press, 1991), pp. 89, 74, 73.

Most residents of the Republic of Texas favored joining the United States. In 1845 the Anglo-dominated Texas legislature voted to approve annexation, thereby dissolving the Republic of Texas.

When the United States added Texas as a new state, tensions with Mexico bristled. War soon broke out between the two countries. Most of the fighting took place to the south as U.S. forces marched from Corpus Christi into Mexico. Soldiers arriving by ship at Veracruz mobilized and occupied Mexico City. Forced to accept the victor's terms, Mexico surrendered claims to half its territory, including what are today the states of Texas, New Mexico, Arizona, California, Utah, and parts of Colorado and Wyoming. Mexico also agreed to recognize the Rio Grande River as the southern boundary of Texas. With the agreement, the westernmost towns of Socorro, Ysleta, and San Elizario became part of the new Texas state.

The signing of the Treaty of Guadalupe Hidalgo on February 2, 1848, ended the war with Mexico. Today some Mexican Americans celebrate Segundo de Febrero to mark the day they first became citizens of the United States.

Texas changed political jurisdiction two more times in the following years. During the American Civil War, Texas withdrew from the Union to join the Confederate States of America. Following the Confederacy's defeat, Texas again was incorporated into the United States. The Civil War affected the fortunes of merchants, politicians, and slave owners in Texas. For Mexican Texans, the outcome of these midcentury struggles placed the future of Texas firmly in American hands. Dominant customs and influences would be coming from the United States, not Mexico. Mexico never again sought to exercise political control over Texas.

THE ECONOMIC LANDSCAPE. Anglo-Americans now pushed to the far corners of the state, building towns and businesses. By the 1860s they were moving into the Cross Timbers of north-central Texas and on to the Panhandle. The building of railroads across Texas accelerated this settlement and spurred economic develop-

Ignacio Zaragoza, 1829–62.
Institute of Texan Cultures
illustration no. 75-1295

ment. San Antonio grew into a prosperous commercial center, the largest city in the state.

Mexican Texans remained a significant population along the length of the Rio Grande and in Central Texas within the old San Antonio–Goliad corridor. Most of them, about three-fourths, lived in rural areas, but many no longer owned the lands they worked.

Tejanos lost title to their lands in a variety of ways. Many in

Ignacio Zaragoza, a Hero of Two Nations

On May 5, 1862, Ignacio Zaragoza defeated invading French troops near Puebla, Mexico. His victory created a groundswell of Mexican national pride.

Ironically, Zaragoza had been born in Texas. His father had emigrated from Veracruz, Mexico, to serve as a soldier near San Antonio. His mother was a native of San Antonio and relative of Juan Seguín. Following Texas independence, the Zaragozas, like many other Spanish-speaking families, withdrew to Mexico.

Fifteen-year-old Ignacio entered a seminary in Monterrey in 1844. Finding himself ill suited for the priesthood, he left the seminary. He volunteered to help defend Mexico when U.S. troops invaded in 1846. This

Vendors arrive at 6:00 A.M. to sell their wares at the Mexican market on Military Plaza, San Antonio, 1884. Anglo businesses around the market now dominate commerce. Institute of Texan Cultures illustration no. 83-85

Central Texas had been driven off their land following the Texas Revolution of 1836. Inhabitants of other regions found their property contested when Americans moved into the area. Some struggled with the English language and complexities of the American legal system, not understanding how to file a land claim. Swindlers and land speculators abounded. Lacking cash, Tejano ranchers were vulnerable to market downturns and weather calamities. Some sold out to pay taxes while other rancheros subdivided their land among heirs until no parcel remained large enough to support their families.

Despite the difficulties, a few Tejanos managed to hold onto their lands in the late nineteenth century and to expand them. Several Tejano ranches spread over the plains of Texas' southeastern tip, especially in Zapata, Webb, Starr, and Duval Counties. Some of these functioned as small villages, with a church, school, store, and housing for their laborers. During the cattle boom, rancheros did business with out-of-state agents and sold animals to trail drivers who transported them north.

In South Texas a solid majority of the population was of Mexican descent. Anglos who moved in succeeded in gaining a good deal of political and economic control, but they depended upon cooperation from the local inhabitants. In this region, more than in any other, intermarriage and godparenting were used to cement alliances. Anglos learned to speak Spanish, married into Tejano families, and developed business partnerships with in-laws. Anglo ranch owners commonly lived in a Spanish-style dwelling and adopted a "Mexicanized" lifestyle.

Virtually all ranchers, whether Tejano or Anglo, hired Tejano laborers when available. Tejanos earned an unmatched reputation as stock handlers, their skills perfected from generations on the range and in the saddle. "For this business [taming horses]," wrote a publicist, "there is no nation in the world superior to the Spaniards of Texas."[17]

In the final decades of the nineteenth century, cattle prices fell and ranching waned. Commercial farms began to replace ranches in Texas. Laborers faced a transition from being ranch hands who

offer was rejected, but shortly afterward, Zaragoza began to rise in the ranks of the Mexican army. In the Mexican constitutional struggle of the 1850s, he supported the reform efforts of Benito Juárez and opposed Santa Anna.

Aware of Mexico's disunity and internal weakness, European powers seized the opportunity to intervene. France, England, and Spain sent military forces to Mexico late in 1861. The United States, embroiled in its own Civil War, was helpless to prevent this activity. European powers could potentially have supplied the Confederacy from Mexico.

Suffering from personal tragedy—the deaths of his wife and three of their four children—Ignacio Zaragoza mustered his forces near Puebla and defeated invading

French troops in a pitched battle on May 5, 1862. His countrymen celebrated wildly and hailed him as a hero. Yet just four months after his famous victory, Zaragoza died of typhoid at age 33.

Today Zaragoza stands as a symbol of idealism and perseverance. The Battle of Puebla is honored on May 5 in both Mexico and Texas. Mexico marks the date as a national holiday. Tejanos organize civic ceremonies in various Texas towns—especially at Goliad, Zaragoza's birthplace.

Source: "Zaragoza, Ignacio Seguín," *The Handbook of Texas Online*, http://www.tsha.utexas.edu/handbook/online/articles/view/ZZ/fza4.html (Nov. 13, 2001), hereinafter cited as HOT Online.

A Mexican horseman in the rain. From a book published in Paris in 1862. Institute of Texan Cultures illustration no. 74-384

worked stock to being farmhands who picked vegetables and cotton. Families first began to follow the cotton crops in the 1890s. They would harvest early ripening crops in the warm parts of the state, then move to cool parts of the state for later ripening crops.

About one-fourth of Tejanos lived in towns. Tejanos tended to reside either in an all-Mexican community or in a separate neighborhood *(barrio)* in a larger Anglo town. Though Tejanos were segregated, this arrangement helped to bring people together and to preserve aspects of their culture. Teachers, druggists, notaries, and shopkeepers emerged to serve their neighborhood. Tejano craftsmen plied their skills as shoemakers, blacksmiths, stonemasons, and carpenters. Spanish-language newspapers first appeared in the 1850s. These publications kept residents informed of both local affairs and events in Mexico.

Feliciana and Pedro López with their youngest child, Carlota, ca. 1906. Institute of Texan Cultures illustration no. 96-106

The foremost gathering place for the Tejano community was the local market. Here people could purchase fruits and vegetables and familiar products: tamales, earthenware pots, wicker birdcages, pecan pralines, and more. San Antonio became famous for its open-air chili stands, where spicy bowls of beans and meat were sold by firelight.

Anglo customers as well as Tejanos stopped by to purchase chili after work. Tejano entrepreneurs and a small class of professionals had contacts with Anglos in the course of doing business. They acquired the skills and knowledge needed to succeed in the broad mainstream society.

THE POLITICAL LANDSCAPE. In areas where Tejanos were a numerical majority, they won election to local offices throughout the latter half of the nineteenth century. This was especially true in the ranching region between the Nueces River and the Rio Grande and in the West Texas villages of Ysleta and San Elizario. In Laredo

▼▼▼

Feliciana Adame López, Ranchwoman

With grit and perseverance, Feliciana Adame participated in a successful ranching enterprise while parenting a large family. She was born in 1863 on a ranch in Tamaulipas, Mexico. Her father owned a piece of land in South Texas. While still a girl, she met Pedro López, son of immigrant ranchers in Duval County. Shortly after her fifteenth birthday, Feliciana became Pedro's bride.

The young couple moved into a jacal on the ranch of Pedro's parents. Feliciana set up housekeeping inside the hut of branches and grasses. Over time Feliciana and Pedro became the parents of twelve children. When one of their daughters died as a young mother, Feliciana and Pedro took in their grandson

Chili vendor in Military Plaza, San Antonio, ca. 1888. Institute of Texan Cultures illustration no. 83-477

and Duval County, parties known as the Botas (boots) and Guaraches (sandals) vied with each other for control.

Much of South Texas adopted a "boss" system, in which a respected ranch owner registered his workers. Out of loyalty to him, workers voted for candidates of his choice. Tejanos sometimes joined with Anglos in operating the boss system. Most of them came from old elite families, concerned with protecting their status and property.

In many areas of the state, people of Mexican heritage joined together to resist ethnic slurs and economic loss. Conflicts sometimes erupted into violence. In 1857 Anglo freighters tried to gain control from Tejano cartmen who transported goods between Central Texas and the Gulf Coast. The Anglos ambushed and destroyed cargoes and killed some drivers. The so-called Cart War ended through the intervention of both the United States and Mexican governments.

In 1857 Juan Cortina, a leader of the Brownsville community, quarreled with the city marshal whom he found insulting a Tejano ranch hand. The argument left the lawman wounded and Cortina on the run. Cortina rallied local supporters and led a raid on

▼▼▼

Brownsville, killing three people. From his mother's ranch, he issued proclamations urging inhabitants to rise and defend themselves against Anglo intruders: "Mexicans! . . . Flocks of vampires, in the guise of men, came and scattered themselves in the settlements. . . . Many of you have been robbed of your property, incarcerated, chased, murdered, and hunted like wild beasts, because your labor was fruitful."[18]

Cortina coordinated further attacks from his stronghold in Cameron County, but ultimately Texas Rangers and U.S. troops drove him into Mexico. Anglos living along the border then took revenge by inflicting violence on suspected sympathizers.[19]

In the El Paso area, residents had always taken whatever salt they needed from the local salt beds. They considered salt to be common property, but a group of Anglos conspired to put the salt lodes under private ownership. In 1877 members of the Salt Ring killed a spokesman for the local Tejanos. Angry residents responded by fighting. Federal troops, Texas Rangers, and posses arrived to stop the disturbance. In the aftermath of the "Salt War," as had been the case following other conflicts, innocent Tejanos suffered acts of violence and death. Residents lost their access to the salt beds.

Oxen haul wool to market, Dimmit County, late 1880s. Institute of Texan Cultures illustration no. 88-61

and raised him, too.

In the early days of their marriage, Feliciana's husband Pedro eagerly rode the range with his brothers. The adventurers rounded up wild mustangs and sold them at markets in San Antonio, Monterrey, Corpus Christi, and Mier. Later they organized cattle drives, purchasing cattle from local ranchers and herding them to stockyards in San Antonio and Houston. Feliciana stayed behind to manage the ranch.

With his earnings, Pedro purchased land in the countryside, some as cheap as fifty cents an acre. When cotton became a cash crop, much of the newly expanded ranch was cleared for cotton growing.

After the trail drives ended, life became more settled. But the work for ranchwomen remained enormous. Feliciana

▼▼▼

remade the old mattresses, replacing cornshuck stuffing with cotton. During sheepshearing time, she carded wool. At hog butchering, she produced chorizo (sausage) and chicharrones (fried rinds of fat). She raised chickens and gathered eggs. She tended the garden crops of corn, beans, onions, and garlic. Corn was a mainstay of their diet, and Feliciana made it into corn tamales, corn bread, corn pudding, and corn cookies.

Feliciana was largely responsible for spiritual health on the ranch. When the Catholic priest made his monthly visits, she hosted him and prepared his meals. Pedro had encounters with what he called la voz del cielo—mysterious warnings of impending danger or reproaches for deeds left undone. The family

Juan Nepomuceno Cortina, 1866. Institute of Texan Cultures illustration no. 92-193

The border region remained unstable through much of the late nineteenth century. Roving groups of bandits—both Mexican and Anglo—attacked ranches and captured livestock. Peaceful settlers found themselves blamed for raids that originated in Mexico. Anglo sheriffs and marshals, often bolstered by the Texas Rangers, represented the final authority. They could jail and hunt down Mexicans as they saw fit. Tejano suspects died in custody under questionable circumstances—"while attempting to escape" or "from self-defense." No eyewitnesses came forward to confirm these reports.

Lynchings occurred. For example, in 1874 a Goliad County mob lynched Juan Moya and his two sons for supposedly killing a white man. A few days later, peace officers captured the real killers and established the Moyas' innocence.[20]

In areas where Tejanos were the majority, some held law-enforcement jobs—serving as sheriff, deputy, jailer, and more. This could put them in the position of pursuing or arresting other Mexican Texans. Tejano elected officials were among the lawmen who chased Catarino Garza in 1891–92.

Catarino Garza was a bold South Texas newspaperman. He published articles criticizing Anglo lawmen suspected of lynching Mexicans. In 1888 an American shot and wounded Garza. Tejano citizens of Rio Grande City rose to the editor's defense, causing a near riot. Garza recovered from his wound to resume his journalist career. In 1891 he began writing editorials against the Mexican dictator Porfirio Díaz. Garza attempted to lead an army of volunteers to unseat Díaz, but American forces crossed into Mexico to halt his advance. Back in Texas, Garza continued to plan rebellion from his father-in-law's ranch in Duval County. U.S. officials moved against him, but the local populace shielded Garza and spirited him to safe lodging. Admired for his commitment and courage, Catarino Garza later became a hero of *corridos,* or popular ballads.

In San Antonio, Tejanos held a handful of political offices in the mid-nineteenth century. They launched rallies against the

took Pedro's messages seriously and hastened to put things right. Feliciana and Pedro sometimes went to see "El Profesor," a man who claimed to have conversations with the dead. Once, El Profesor held a séance in their home.

Feliciana and Pedro were friends with Don Pedrito Jaramillo, the famed folk healer. He told them where to dig a well to find water. When a daughter had nightmares about a panther in her bed, Don Pedrito's prayers dispelled the apparition.

After Pedro's death in 1929, Feliciana expanded the ranching operation, buying more land and building new structures. She died in 1952 at the age of 89.

Source: Andrés Sáenz, *Early Tejano Ranching in Duval County: The Family History of Ranchos San José and El Fresnillo,* ed. Andrés Tijerina (San Antonio: Institute of Texan Cultures, 1999).

▼▼▼

*Catarino Garza, journalist
and revolutionist, 1894.*
Institute of Texan Cultures
illustration no. 70-232

anti-immigrant Know-Nothing Party. But as Anglo-Americans continued to move into the city, Tejanos lost their positions in local politics. By 1900 they lacked representatives in city hall.

THE CULTURAL LANDSCAPE. Many Mexican Texans faced poverty struggling to feed and clothe their families. They lived in simple houses built of materials gathered from the land. In West Texas and other dry areas, they built houses of adobe, mud-and-straw bricks dried in the sun. Roofs were a flat wooden latticework with channels for drainage. Thick adobe walls provided remarkable insulation, keeping the inside warm in winter and cool in summer.

In wetter areas, rain would return adobe to mud, so Tejanos of limited means lived in jacales. A *jacal* is a hut made from readily found materials such as mesquite posts. To build a jacal, family members laid the logs side by side and chinked the spaces in between with mud. Then they raised a peaked roof frame above the

Woman and children outside their jacal, *San Antonio, ca. 1886.* Institute of Texan Cultures illustration no. 83-100

walls, thatching it with bundles of local grasses. Finally, they packed dirt to make a floor. Jacales were vulnerable to insects and windy weather. As families could afford it, they constructed wooden board-and-batten homes, while the most prosperous Tejanos lived in substantial *sillar* block homes of local stone. Some of these stone houses can still be seen today in South Texas.

Mexican Texans cultivated plants around their homes. A vegetable garden could yield corn, beans, tomatoes, peppers, onions, melons, and squash. A small area of the garden was reserved for medicinal herbs: *cenizo* to make cough medicine, *hierbabuena* for heart ailments, *ruda* for earaches, and *manzanilla* to create a calming tea.

Curanderos, or folk healers, ministered to the Tejano population. They treated ailments with a combination of herbs and spiritual practices. The most famous *curandero,* Don Pedrito Jaramillo, attracted an enormous following in South Texas. He migrated from Mexico in 1881 to establish himself at Los Olmos (Brooks County), where he practiced until his death in 1907. Thousands of Mexican Texans made the pilgrimage to Los Olmos for treatment. A shrine to Don Pedrito remains in Falfurrias today.

Local ordinances in the 1870s forbade fandangos, the time-honored, exuberant dance of Spanish-speaking Texans. Tejanos turned to a slightly more sedate version known as the *baile.* In many bailes, no alcohol was served. On ranches the baile could be the social highlight of the year. A newspaper described one such occasion in the El Paso Valley in 1898:

> Charley Peacock, who is in charge of the ranch, decided upon a *baile* to keep the help. Invitations were carefully written out in Spanish and delivered by special messenger. . . . When the girls began to arrive, they brought their ordinary clothes and carried their party clothes with them. As soon as they arrived, they sent to the store for hairpins and vaseline. They went to the homes of the Mexican laborers and began to make ready for the ball. . . . The music consisted of a violin, guitar, and cornet. . . . The dancing continued after that with

no intermission longer than five or ten minutes until long after sunrise. The candles flickered in the early dawn and went out, but still the dancers sailed on.[21]

Tejanos of high social standing entertained separately from laborers. In San Antonio and elsewhere, they held musical recitals and formal balls, dancing to the waltz, quadrille, schottische, and polka.

Fiestas and ferias took place at various times of year. Tejanos traveled from ranches into town, eager to enjoy outdoor refreshments, booths, games of chance, exhibits, and acrobatic performances. Two of the most fervent celebrations were those celebrating the Mexican national holidays of Diez y Seis, when Father Hidalgo issued his cry for independence on September 16, 1810, and Cinco de Mayo, when Ignacio Zaragoza defeated French troops at the Battle of Puebla on May 5, 1862. Festivities included flags, flowers,

The beer wagon float sponsored by Nasario Peña's saloon for Diez y Seis, San Diego, Texas, ca. 1905. Nasario stands on the right in front of his sillar *home on the plaza.* Institute of Texan Cultures illustration no. 96-1218.

Members of Sociedad Benito Juárez gather in Brownsville for the fifty-year anniversary of their organization, 1928. Institute of Texan Cultures illustration no. 73-850

fireworks, and parades of decorated floats. Bands played anthems, and local dignitaries gave patriotic speeches. Border cities staged events in conjunction with sister cities across the Rio Grande. Anglo officials joined with Tejano leaders in organizing marches and reciting Father Hidalgo's *grito*.

As United States citizens, Tejanos also celebrated U.S. holidays like the Fourth of July. Laredo first publicly commemorated George Washington's birthday in February, 1896. Tejanos chose to honor the first U.S. president because a century earlier, George Washington had belonged to the same fraternal association that many Laredoans were joining in the 1890s—Order of the Redman. The festivity met with an enthusiastic response and expanded into an annual event. Today, George Washington Days include a weeklong series of parades, balls, carnivals, and an international bridge ceremony affirming friendship between the United States and Mexico.

In the closing decades of the nineteenth century, Tejanos from many walks of life enrolled in *mutualistas,* or mutual aid societies. These fraternal organizations filled a variety of roles. They functioned as a kind of insurance company, aiding members who suffered illness or funeral expenses. They fostered a sense of belonging and group identity, providing a forum where people could discuss issues of the day. Many mutualistas supported charities and social work. For instance, in 1892 the Sociedad Unión of San Antonio sponsored a dance to raise funds for drought victims on the Mexican border.[22]

The Tejano associations tended to take their names from Mexican heroes and causes. Among the mutualistas in Texas were Sociedad Benito Juárez, Sociedad México-Tejana, Sociedad Mutualista Hijos de Hidalgo, Sociedad Beneficencia (founded by women), Sociedad Ignacio Allende, and Sociedad Ignacio Zaragoza. Leaders from the Tejano community typically started the mutualistas—prominent citizens such as newspapermen, merchants, doctors, and lawyers. They conducted meetings in Spanish, giving emphasis to Mexican heritage and values. At the same time, members sought ways to function more effectively in the United States. As major sponsors of civic celebrations, the mutualistas brought circuses and *carpas* (Mexican tent shows) to rural towns. These performances, which combined acrobatic feats with dramatic presentations, were enthusiastically attended throughout South Texas.

CHAPTER 3
In the Matrix of Modern Texas, 1900–60

*T*HE TWENTIETH CENTURY ushered in new inventions and machines. Texas as a whole grew industrialized, with its population increasingly concentrated in cities. The Lower Rio Grande Valley was given over to commercial farming. The Mexican Revolution of 1910 to 1920 brought new waves of immigrants. Discrimination increased. Tejanos were segregated in housing and schools. Those finding work in fields and factories struggled to survive with low wages.

During the 1930s, organizations and labor unions pressed for change. Large numbers of Tejanos served in World War II. On their return, they qualified for the GI Bill and were able to purchase homes and enroll in higher education. They joined organizations such as the League of Latin American Citizens and the GI Forum and brought issues of discrimination to national attention.

With the passage of the Voting Rights Act of 1965, Tejanos increasingly won election to public office. Today, Tejanos with a range of political views serve at local, state, and national levels.

Tejanos are a part of mainstream society yet maintain a distinct identity through their language, food, music, celebrations, and family ties. This identity, which has never been static, continues to evolve.

Mexican workers laying railroad ties between Dunlay and Medina Dam, 1911. Institute of Texan Cultures illustration no. 88-177

USHERING IN A NEW ERA, 1900–30

From 1890 until the Great Depression of 1929, an estimated 1.5 million people entered Texas from Mexico.[1] The first wave of immigrants fled the political and economic tyranny of Porfirio Díaz. During the Mexican Revolution from 1910 to 1920, people sought to escape feuding factions and dangers to life and property.

Texas, meanwhile, was experiencing an economic boom. Jobs in Texas beckoned. Crossing the Rio Grande, immigrants encountered Tejanos whose families had lived in Texas for generations. Sometimes the old families welcomed the newcomers like long-lost brothers. Other times there was distrust between Tejanos, who were U.S. citizens, and Mexican immigrants, who were not.

▼▼▼

While Mexicans came from the south, another group of immigrants moved to Texas from the north—Anglo farmers from the U.S. Midwest pushed into the Lower Rio Grande Valley. They brought money to invest and began purchasing land from Tejanos who needed cash. Within a few short years, the Anglo investors had transformed old ranch lands into commercial farms. Small family-owned ranches nearly disappeared, with remnants surviving in a few counties like Duval and Starr.

WORKING THE TEXAS BOOM. A network of railroad tracks, laid between 1880 and the early 1900s, connected Texas cities. Following the Spindletop oil discovery in 1901, Houston grew into a major oil and gas production center. Some of the new arrivals from Mexico took jobs in the oilfields, on the railroads, or on construction projects. They settled in towns that had previously seen little Mexican presence, like Houston, Dallas, and Fort Worth.

The majority of jobs lay in agriculture. Commercial farmers needed a steady source of cheap labor. For field hands, they turned to the Mexican population, many of whom would work in poor conditions for low wages. Growers made little distinction between U.S.-born Tejanos and recent immigrants, referring to both groups as "Mexicans."

Growers secured the passage of local ordinances to prevent workers from leaving the country during critical times of planting or harvest. When there was no work to be done, the growers expelled the hired hands from their property. Some counties prohibited Mexican children from attending school beyond sixth grade.[2] A grower explained the need to keep potential workers away from school: "Educating the Mexicans is educating them away from the job, away from the dirt. He learns English and wants to be a boss. He doesn't want to grub."[3]

A small number of Tejanos farmed as sharecroppers. Sharecroppers lived on the property of a landowner and were allowed to keep a percentage, typically 50 percent, of the crop they cultivated. More commonly, farmworkers followed the harvest.

▼▼▼

Matilde Elizondo, Entrepreneur

Like thousands of others, Matilde Elizondo immigrated to Texas during the tumult of the Mexican Revolution. He was seventeen in 1914, when his parents sent him north to avoid the fighting. In San Antonio Matilde met and married Aurelia Herrera, whose family made a harrowing escape from Mexico after her father's name appeared on a death list.

Matilde began work as a grocery clerk earning three dollars a week. When he had saved one hundred dollars, he sent it to his parents in Nuevo León so they could join him. By 1918 he had earned another one hundred dollars, enough to open his own grocery store. The Elizondo family later operated additional businesses: a gas station, a roof garden for neighborhood dances, a

Cotton—known as "King Cotton"—was the most profitable crop. Cotton grew well in many parts of Texas, ripening first in the south, then in Central Texas, and last in western regions of El Paso and the Panhandle. When harvest ended, families typically returned to San Antonio or another South Texas town for the winter. Some families decided to stay in the final area worked during the season. Tejano farmworkers began to settle in Panhandle towns of Lubbock, Plainview, Muleshoe, and Tahoka.

Hostility toward immigrants mounted. Some Americans grew alarmed at the number of Mexicans coming across the border. They pushed for a series of restrictive immigration laws following World War I. In 1928 the Texas government began enforcing the laws—an action that effectively closed the border to further immigration.

CITIZENS OF *MÉXICO DE AFUERA*. Most immigrants arriving from Mexico were unskilled laborers. However, a small cadre of intellectuals, professionals, and businessmen also fled the turmoil of the Mexican Revolution. In Texas, they operated printing presses, opened retail shops, and worked as doctors, lawyers, and teachers.

Many of this influx of middle-class and laboring people, who came to be known as the immigrant generation, planned to return to Mexico when conditions settled. Immigrants retained ties to their hometowns. Some organized relief efforts for compatriots who remained in Mexico.

In urban areas, Mexican Texans typically lived in a specific part of town with its own barbershops, restaurants, drugstores, and bookstores. Store signs were in Spanish, and people spoke Spanish when conducting business. The surroundings seemed so much like Mexico that inhabitants thought of themselves as living in México *de afuera*—"Mexico from afar."

They also were living in segregation. This isolation increased with time. In 1902 Texas established the first school exclusively for Mexicans. Ninety percent of Texas schools were segregated by 1930.[4] To justify separation, supporters and planners spread the idea that

Matilde Elizondo (right) checks supplies inside the warehouse of his San Antonio store, 1922. Courtesy of Patti Elizondo. Institute of Texan Cultures illustration no. 98-1120

pecan orchard, and an early trailer park, opened when World War II brought temporary residents to Kelly Field.

Throughout his life Matilde Elizondo made annual trips to his hometown of Villa del Carmen, Mexico. A welcomed and honored guest, he took part in a special mass, purchased a steer to feed the community, and bestowed awards on schoolchildren.

All five of Matilde and Aurelia's children grew up to be successful Texas professionals and entrepreneurs. Matilde died in 1949 at age fifty-two.

Sources: Interviews with Patricia Elizondo and Rosalinda Elizondo, Institute of Texan Cultures; "A Family Album: From Revolution to Prosperity," *San Antonio Express-News*, Sept. 16, 1990, 1–2K; Oscar Elizondo, "Biography of Matilde Elizondo," unpublished manuscript, Institute of Texan Cultures library.

"Mexicans are dirty." They pointed to poor housing and other conditions of poverty in arguing this claim.

Tejano parents struggled to provide adequate education for their children. In 1910 they boycotted San Angelo schools, protesting segregation and the limited instruction for Tejanos. For the next several years, 1910–15, these parents enrolled their children in either the local Catholic school or a Mexican Presbyterian school. Parents in Big Wells withdrew their children from the local Mexican schools in 1929, insisting they would keep them away "until we get a teacher with a better disposition toward the Mexicans."[5]

Despite segregation and discrimination, Mexican Texans preserved their cultural identity. Immigrants and native Texans alike joined in celebrating *fiestas patrias*. They competed to build the most elaborate float for the local parade. Border folk ballads called *corridos*

Tejano students outside their segregated school in Dilley, Texas, 1920s. Institute of Texan Cultures illustration no. 96-37

told of heroes who performed deeds of resistance, gallantry, valor, or loyalty.

Music had always played a major role in Tejano culture. During this period, songs of northern Mexico found wide popularity in Texas. Anastacia Sáenz, growing up in rural Duval County around 1920, recalled her brothers sharing their music with the neighbors: "Three members of the family were musicians, Praxidis, Eleuterio and Eustorgio. They would play in dances, weddings, and sometimes after the dances someone wanted to go serenade a relative. . . . They would get home around 3:00 A.M., and had to get up and work the fields the next day."[6]

MEXICAN AMERICAN VOTERS. Although their parents sought to preserve a distinct culture, a new generation of immigrant children grew up in the United States—and grew accustomed to its habits. They easily learned English. Both public and parochial schools taught loyalty to the United States. Theaters in Mexican neighborhoods screened both Mexican and U.S. films. When World War I broke out, Tejanos supported and endorsed the U.S. war effort. They were eager to prove their patriotism.

Many in the immigrant generation intended to move back to Mexico someday. In actuality, most never did. They merged with Tejano neighbors and became permanent residents of their adopted country. Their children born in Texas were American citizens.

A movement began to deny the vote to both old-time Tejanos and Mexican immigrants. Anglo farmers were anxious to break up the "boss system" that determined the outcome of elections. In farm counties, activists succeeded in establishing White Men's Primary Associations and the poll tax, which required a cash payment to vote. Many Mexican Texans could not afford the poll tax and stopped voting.

In many urban areas, citywide elections replaced the earlier ward system. No longer able to elect a resident from their barrio, Tejanos lost any representation in city government.

In a few remaining ranch counties, Tejanos succeeded in winning elections, but they gained access only to local offices. J. T. Canales of Brownsville served in the Texas legislature from 1905 to 1910 and again from 1916 to 1920. He took stands in support of women's suffrage and opposed efforts to restrict Tejano voters. Canales was the last Mexican American in the state legislature until the late 1930s.[7]

WINDS OF VIOLENCE. Seeking to protect themselves and oppose injustices, Mexican Texans sometimes participated in violent confrontations. In 1901, in the midst of a quarrel, Gregorio Cortez fired upon a local sheriff near Kenedy in Karnes County. Fearing he would be lynched for wounding the lawman, Cortez fled across Texas toward Mexico. Sympathetic Tejanos offered him food and horses along the way, but Texas Rangers caught up with him after ten days. Cortez was imprisoned but not executed; the governor of Texas pardoned him in 1913. His daring flight became a legend and the topic of *corridos:*

Venían los perros jaunes,	They set bloodhounds on him,
venían sobre la huella,	So they could follow his trail,
pero alcanzar a Cortez	But trying to overtake Cortez
era seguir a una estrella.	Was like following a star.
Decía Gregorio Cortez:	Then said Gregorio Cortez,
Con su pistola en la mano:	With his pistol in his hand,
—No siento haberte matado,	"I don't regret that I killed him;
lo que siento es a mi hermano.	I regret my brother's death."[8]

Texas became a safe haven for Mexican nationals embroiled in the Mexican Revolution. Ricardo Flores Magón, a Mexican intellectual, arrived in Texas in 1904 to establish a political party and printing press. He called for the overthrow of Mexican dictator Porfirio Díaz and urged Tejanos to support their countrymen in Mexico. Flores Magón's political party welcomed women into its ranks. The writer Sara Estela Ramírez joined his cause and organized workers along the Texas border from 1904 until her death in 1910.

Francisco Madero, later president of Mexico, planned details of the revolution from exile in San Antonio. In 1911 his forces captured the city of Juárez on the U.S.-Mexico border. Madero's early victories caused Díaz to resign and flee to Paris, but Madero himself was assassinated two years later. After Madero's death, rivals in Mexico fought for power and control of the government. Some leaders profited from intrigue and sought support from the United States. Venustiano Carranza encouraged raids in Texas as a way to gain leverage for diplomatic recognition. Pancho Villa attacked trains in northern Mexico, killing Americans. Early in 1916 his forces looted Columbus, New Mexico, a town just across the state line from El Paso. This brash act prompted a punitive expedition into Mexico led by Gen. John Pershing.

The Mexican Revolution frayed the nerves of people living along the border. Landholders suspected their employees of harboring revolutionary sympathies. Resentment and class tensions simmered among Tejanos who had lost their land or livelihood. Tensions peaked in 1915 with the signing of the Plan de San Diego, named for the South Texas town. The Plan de San Diego called upon Mexican Americans and Native Americans to rise up and retake the original Spanish Southwest and create from it an independent republic. In response to the plan's call to arms, scattered groups of bandits began to attack Anglo ranches and businesses in Texas and to sabotage equipment. When raiders attacked a division of the King Ranch, Texas Rangers came out in force, killing Mexicans and Mexican Texans indiscriminately. At least one hundred—possibly more than three hundred—people died in the immediate aftermath. Five thousand Mexicans and Mexican Texans may have died in Texas during the years of the Mexican Revolution.[9]

The *ley de fuga* (law of flight) was used to explain deaths of unarmed prisoners. In its September 15, 1915, issue, the *San Antonio Express* newspaper reported that "[t]hree Mexicans among six prisoners taken on suspicion after the Los Indios fight yesterday were

Nicasio Idar, Laredo newspaperman, ca. 1910. Nicasio was a devout Methodist and a Mason. Institute of Texan Cultures illustration no. 100-636

Jovita Idar: Nurse, Teacher, Journalist

Jovita Idar, born in Laredo in 1885, was the second of nine children in the Idar family of journalists. She grew up in a household dedicated to defending the poor and promoting justice. At age seventeen, she received a teaching certificate from the Holding Institute and immediately set about teaching Tejano children in the small town of Ojuelos.

But Jovita was frustrated by the conditions around her—children exhausted from poverty, insufficient heat in the school building, and not enough chairs and desks for the students who tried to attend. Deciding that she could be more effective as a journalist, Jovita returned to Laredo and joined her two brothers in writing for her father's newspaper, La Crónica. She

killed today near San Benito. It was stated that they escaped from the San Benito jail during the night, and that their bodies were found some distance from town today with bullet holes in their backs."

After major loss of life and property, the raids from Mexico ceased. President Carranza of Mexico achieved diplomatic recognition from the United States and withdrew his support for the attackers. The Plan de San Diego withered, its goals unachieved. The legacy of border violence was a hardening of attitudes and a tightening of restrictions on Mexican Texans.

SEEDS OF CHANGE. Throughout the opening decades of the twentieth century, Mexican Texans organized to improve their lives. Shunned by national labor unions like the American Federation of Labor (AFL), they founded their own unions. Mutualistas, mutual aid societies patterned after those in Mexico, continued to thrive. Women served as officers and even founders of Texas mutualistas.

Tejano workers participated in strikes against the El Paso Street Car Company in 1901. They demonstrated against severe conditions at the Thurber mines in the 1890s and 1926. Following World War I, national labor organizations began to take notice of Tejano workers. The AFL employed Clemente Idar to travel the state and organize workers.

Clemente Idar was the son of influential Laredo newspaperman Nicasio Idar, who advocated Tejano unity. Together with his young-adult children, Nicasio published *La Crónica* newspaper in the early 1900s. The journalist team fearlessly wrote articles denouncing the lynchings, inferior education, cultural dilution, and loss of land. In 1911 *La Crónica* called for a conference to discuss concerns of Mexican Texans. Participants in this "First Mexican Congress" founded leagues dedicated to protecting Tejanos and preserving traditions.

In the 1920s, several organizations arose that sought to project Tejanos as loyal citizens and to promote their acceptance into American life. These groups included Orden Hijos de América in 1921, Caballeros de América in 1927, and most important, the League of United Latin American Citizens (LULAC) in 1929. With their

JANUARY		APRIL	
S	1 8 15 22 29	S	2 9 16 23
M	2 9 16 23 30	M	3 10 17 24
Tu	3 10 17 24 31	Tu	4 11 18 25
W	4 11 18 25	W	5 12 19 26
Th	5 12 19 26	Th	6 13 20 27
F	6 13 20 27	F	7 14 21 28
S	7 14 21 28	S	1 8 15 22 29

MAY		JUNE	
S	7 14 21 28	S	4 11 18 25
M	1 8 15 22 29	M	5 12 19 26
Tu	2 9 16 23 30	Tu	6 13 20 27
W	3 10 17 24 31	W	7 14 21 28
Th	4 11 18 25	Th	1 8 15 22 29
F	5 12 19 26	F	2 9 16 23 30
S	6 13 20 27	S	3 10 17 24

FEBRUARY	
S	5 12 19 26
M	6 13 20 27
Tu	7 14 21 28
W	1 8 15 22
Th	2 9 16 23
F	3 10 17 24
S	4 11 18 25

JULY	
S	2 9 16
M	3 10 17
Tu	4 11 18 25
W	5 12 19 26
Th	6 13 20 27
F	7 14 21 28
S	1 8 15 22 29

MARCH	
S	5 12 19 26
M	6 13 20 27
Tu	7 14 21 28
W	1 8 15 22 29
Th	2 9 16 23 30
F	3 10 17 24 31
S	4 11 18 25

AUGUST	
S	6 13 20 27
M	7 14 21 28
Tu	1 8 15 22 29
W	2 9 16 23 30
Th	3 10 17 24 31
F	4 11 18 25
S	5 12 19 26

SEPTEMBER	
S	3 10 17 24
M	4 11 18 25
Tu	5 12 19 26
W	6 13 20 27
Th	7 14 21 28
F	1 8 15 22 29
S	2 9 16 23 30

NOVEMBER	
S	5 12 19 26
M	6 13 20 27
Tu	7 14 21 28
W	1 8 15 22 29
Th	2 9 16 23 30
F	3 10 17 24
S	4 11 18 25

OCTOBER	
S	1 8 15 22 29
M	2 9 16 23 30
Tu	3 10 17 24 31
W	4 11 18 25
Th	5 12 19 26
F	6 13 20 27
S	7 14 21 28

DECEMBER	
S	3 10 17
M	4 11 18 25
Tu	5 12 19 26
W	6 13 20 27
Th	7 14 21 28
F	1 8 15 22 29
S	2 9 16 23 30

1911

May Every Happiness be Thine This New Year!

X·S·11070.

ROTARY PHOTO E.C.

Jovita Idar, in a 1911 calendar postcard. Institute of Texan Cultures illustration no. 100-634

expressed outrage at incidents of racial violence—particularly when a fourteen-year-old Tejano child was hauled from jail, beaten to death by a mob, and dragged through the Laredo streets.

When the Idar family arranged the First Mexican Congress, Jovita organized the women who attended. Out of this effort sprang *La Liga Feminil Mexicanista (Mexican Feminist League)*, whose mission was education for Tejano children. Jovita and other members created free elementary school classes and collected food, clothing, and school supplies for the needy.

In 1913 the Mexican Revolution came to the gates of Laredo. Jovita's good friend Leonor Villegas de Magnón appealed to her with a humanitarian mission. Together the two women crossed the river into

▼▼▼

Nuevo Laredo to nurse and rescue the war wounded. They ministered to both revolutionary recruits and government soldiers. Later Leonor founded La Cruz Blanca (the White Cross), an organization similar to the American Red Cross. She and Jovita spent time in revolutionary armies, sharing their healing expertise.

Back in Laredo, Jovita took a position writing for the Spanish-language newspaper El Progreso. *In 1914 the paper published an article criticizing President Wilson for sending U.S. troops to the Mexican border. Incensed by the editorial, four Texas Rangers arrived to close down the print shop. They found Jovita alone. She faced them squarely in the doorway, refusing to let them enter. The Rangers departed, but they returned the next*

emphasis on citizenship, these groups were the foundation for the coming prominence of the Mexican American generation.

THE MEXICAN AMERICAN GENERATION, 1930–60

COPING IN THE GREAT DEPRESSION, 1930–40. The stock market crash of 1929 and the subsequent economic depression of the 1930s brought dire conditions to Tejanos. Many jobs vanished. Farm owners were less inclined to hire migrant labor. Jobless Mexicans crowded into Texas cities, trying to survive in some of the worst slums in the nation.

In San Antonio many of the Mexican people found shelter in *corrales,* wooden shacks surrounding an open space. These houses had no indoor plumbing. The open space contained an outhouse toilet and a spigot for drawing water.

Disease was rampant in the overcrowded housing. People suffered intestinal illnesses and respiratory infections. San Antonio in 1937 had the highest death rate from tuberculosis of any major American city. Among the local Mexican population, 144 babies died for every 1,000 live births.[10] An inspector from the city's health department reported finding a dwelling comprised of "a single room big enough for two beds, the three feet between them occupied by the baby's crib, and a lean-to kitchen almost entirely filled with a small wood stove. This was the home of an expectant mother with moderately advanced tuberculosis, her nineteen-month-old child, and her husband."[11]

Unemployment among Hispanic males ran exceptionally high. Women sought ways to provide income for their families but faced racial and gender stereotyping when seeking jobs. Some sewed infants' clothes or did other handwork from their homes. A contractor supplied raw materials but bought back only the best-quality finished pieces. By the late 1930s, officials pushed to shut down home labor, claiming that products made at home were unsanitary.[12]

▼▼▼

City health nurse gathering data in a Mexican neighborhood, San Antonio, 1936. Institute of Texan Cultures illustration no. 1276C

day when Jovita was away and smashed the printing press, Linotype machine, and wooden table. The newspaper was never able to reopen.

In 1917, at age thirty-two, Jovita married and moved with her husband to San Antonio. There she set up a free kindergarten for Mexican American children, volunteered as a Spanish-language interpreter at the county hospital, and edited a Methodist newspaper. She remained an active educator and voice for reform until her death in 1946.

Sources: "Idar, Jovita," *HOT Online,* http:www.tsha.utexas. edu/handbook/online/articles/ view/II/fid3.html (Aug. 8, 2000); Robin K. Berson, *Marching to a Different Drummer* (Westport, Conn.: Greenwood Press, 1994), pp. 154–56; "Jovita Idar: Por La Raza y Para La Raza," *La Voz de Aztlán* 1, no. 5 (Feb. 27, 2000), http://www.aztlan.net (Feb. 20, 2001); Yolanda Chávez Leyva, "Una Sola Mexicana: Jovita's Story, April 1914," *La Voz de Esperanza* (Sept., 1999): 20–22.

Mexican American mothers were reluctant to leave their homes for work. However, unmarried girls and older women increasingly took factory jobs. In El Paso, Mexican women found work as domestics, laundresses, or seamstresses. In San Antonio, they found jobs in the tobacco, garment, and pecan industries.

Employers placed their factories in Mexican neighborhoods to take advantage of a ready supply of labor. Because so many women were willing to work, employers could pay low wages. In pecan factories, Tejana women spent long hours hunched over tables, tediously picking nutmeats from shells. For this they were paid pennies a pound. One seamstress spent twelve hours hand making a delicate dress at home; a contractor gave her forty-two cents for it and sold it in an Eastern shop for eight dollars.[13] In El Paso, a household paid a domestic worker just fifteen cents a day. From

▼▼▼

that salary she struggled to support her family of five, feeding them only bread.[14]

While wage labor suffered, some Tejanos weathered the Depression as independent entrepreneurs. Mexican sections of town offered grocery stores, Spanish-language printing presses, and pharmacies that sold herbal remedies. Theater houses such as Teatro Nacional in San Antonio brought in entertainers from Mexico, attracting eager audiences. Radio programs broadcast news, commentary, and Mexican songs. Vendors hawked shoes and other wares through the streets of town. Chili stands continued to be a gathering spot for San Antonians, although the city ordered them screened for health reasons in 1936. With this action, the council ended a two-hundred-year tradition of open-air eateries.

Public relief was nonexistent before the New Deal legislation of the mid-1930s. Settlement houses, Catholic and Protestant churches, the Salvation Army, and the International Institute attempted to feed and clothe the poor. LULAC initiated many efforts to boost the Tejano community. Members, both men and women, organized PTAs in barrio schools, taught English, subsidized the education of promising students, served as leaders of Boy Scouts and Girl Scouts, participated in fund-raisers for the Salvation Army and Red Cross, and volunteered in orphanages and health clinics.[15]

With jobs in short supply, immigrants were a lightning rod for attracting blame. A movement arose to "repatriate" them by sending them back to Mexico. Critics charged that immigrants took jobs from Americans, brought disease, and lived in slums. Mexican consuls serving in Texas attempted to assist their countrymen in returning to Mexico. Mexico granted a general amnesty to those who had fled to the United States during the Mexican Revolution.

An estimated 250,000 persons from Texas returned to Mexico during the years 1929 through 1939.[16] Repatriates included many members of mutual aid societies. Mutual aid societies declined in Texas following the loss of their leaders. Their treasuries were drained from helping people in need.[17] Nervously watching the deportations, Tejanos who were United States citizens sought to distinguish them-

Genaro Cantú, dulcero, made coconut and pecan candies on his wood-burning stove and sold them near the Bexar County Courthouse in San Antonio for sixteen years, 1941. Institute of Texan Cultures illustration no. 2853C

selves from recent immigrants. They referred to themselves as Mexican Americans to underscore their citizenship. They resisted the tendency of authorities to look upon all "Mexicans" as alike.

LULAC, which had always emphasized American citizenship, did not oppose the removal of foreigners. However, the organization

Beatrice Denmark, a representative of the National Youth Administration, inspecting a women's sewing room, 1937. Institute of Texan Cultures illustration no. 1534EE

protested strongly in 1936, when the Census Bureau announced plans to classify Mexican Americans as "non-white." Surprised by this strong reaction, the Census Bureau withdrew the classification.[18] LULAC continued to attract new members and grow until World War II, when many of its leaders departed for the armed services.

New Deal legislation in the mid-1930s brought some relief to impoverished Texans. Fear of deportation, however, kept many Mexican Texans from enrolling in its jobs or programs. Most programs trained for jobs segregated by gender or ethnicity—for instance, sewing rooms for young Tejana women. The Works Progress

Administration (WPA) and National Youth Administration (NYA) provided major sources of jobs in the years 1935 to 1939. For many families, a single member participating in a federal program earned the household's sole income.[19]

Federal funds supported Americanization programs. At Sidney Lanier High School in San Antonio, over three hundred Hispanic men and women enrolled in adult education classes in English, citizenship, and trade skills. Women received instruction in nutrition, home management, child care, and clerical training.[20]

The National Labor Relations Act of 1935 gave workers the right to organize and bargain collectively. This spurred a growth in unions, headed by both native Tejanos and outside organizers. Laundry and domestic workers created unions in El Paso during the 1930s. Harvesters in Laredo called a strike on irrigated farms in 1935. However, the most vigorous labor activity took place in San Antonio.

Between 1933 and 1935, an estimated four hundred Tejana women walked off their jobs in a series of strikes against the Finck Cigar Factory in San Antonio. Their grievances included leaking pipes in work areas, ill-equipped bathrooms, and other unsafe conditions. Throughout their protests, the women held rallies and sponsored benefit events. Owners of the company broke the strike by hiring nonunion workers.[21]

The International Ladies' Garment Workers' Union (ILGWU) went to considerable effort to organize garment workers in San Antonio. Most of these workers were Tejana women employed in hand sewing handkerchiefs and children's clothes. In 1936 members of ILGWU struck at the Dorothy Frocks Company. Police arrested strikers for blocking sidewalks and interfering with business. When the company announced the closing of its San Antonio plant, the strike dissolved. The plant later reopened but did not rehire the union leaders.[22]

San Antonio's most bitter and protracted labor struggle arose during the pecan shellers' strike of 1938. Pecan shelling, the least desirable of all factory work, was done almost exclusively by Tejanos. Men did the "cracking," or breaking the shells, while women did the

Emma Tenayuca, Labor Leader

Emma Tenayuca was just sixteen years old in 1932 when she joined a strike of women cigar makers. Born in San Antonio, she grew up in an atmosphere of fervent talk and political action. "I could not help but be impressed by the discussions inside of my family, my family circle. Also, the Plaza del Zacate was the type of place where everyone went on Saturday and Sundays to hold discussions. If you went there, you could find a minister preaching. You could also find revolutionists from Mexico holding discussions. I was exposed to all of this."

By 1937 Emma held a leadership role with the Workers Alliance of America, a group that sought to unite organizations of the unemployed and industrial workers. She delivered fiery speeches to

Two pecan shellers, ages 13 and 77, working in San Antonio in 1938. Institute of Texan Cultures illustration no. 1739F

more tedious work of picking the nutmeat from the shell. In the process, workers cut and bruised their fingers and suffered respiratory illnesses from inhaling particles of pecan dust. Children as young as eight years old worked at the factories. A pecan shelling "factory" might consist of nothing more than a rented shed furnished with wooden tables and benches.[23]

In 1938 companies announced a wage reduction to four cents a pound. Six thousand pecan workers walked away from their jobs—a huge number for a town the size of San Antonio. Twenty-one-year-old Emma Tenayuca rallied the workers with rousing speeches. Several hundred were arrested. The strike gathered wide community support. The Women's International League for Peace and Freedom set up a soup kitchen, feeding over one thousand strikers a day.

During the strike, charges of police misconduct abounded—tear gassing, clubbing, harassment, brutality, and threats of deportation.

▼▼▼

The American Civil Liberties Union (ACLU) sought an injunction to stop the mass arrests, but their request was denied. After weeks of conflict, the strikers won an improved contract of seven cents a pound.

The new wages proved to be disappointing. Small operators responded by closing up shop, while large operators converted to machine shelling. Jobs for pecan shellers fell by 75 percent.[24]

In the end, Tejanos saw little gain from New Deal legislation or from the labor movement of the 1930s. For most Tejanos, the major legacy of the Depression was increased Americanization. Tejanos heard and heeded appeals like those of Charles Porras, a Mexican American labor organizer in El Paso, who urged them to Americanize. "You claim to be Americans, yet you speak the language of Mexicans, so you do not deserve to be classed as anything else but Mexicans. If you are Americans, speak the English language, live like Americans and be proud of it. Teach your children to speak English, bring them up in the knowledge that they are Americans."[25]

Hispanic audiences and led sit-down strikes at the Works Progress Administration (WPA) headquarters and at city hall. Looking back, she explained what drove her to take such dangerous actions: "I carried an Indian name. And I was very, very conscious of that. It was this historical background and my grandparents' attitude which formed my ideas and actually gave me that courage to undertake the type of work I did in San Antonio."

In January, 1938, when pecan shellers in San Antonio walked out of their jobs, they looked to Emma for leadership. She immediately joined them. Their ranks swelled to between six and eight thousand strikers. Emma was arrested and released along with hundreds of others. Then a dispute over leadership arose between the Workers

Emma Tenayuca and Workers Alliance members stage a sit-down protest in San Antonio's City Hall, 1937. Institute of Texan Cultures illustration no. 1541E

Alliance and the Congress of Industrial Organizations (CIO). Emma's communist affiliations were used to discredit her. Although she agreed to take a background role for the duration of the strike, she continued to write fliers and provide support behind the scenes.

In 1939 Emma was meeting with Communist Party members inside the new municipal auditorium. A crowd stormed the building, smashing windows and attacking participants. Emma managed to escape, but she never again led a major labor protest.

Employers blacklisted her. As a result, Emma was unable to find work in San Antonio. She moved to California in 1946, where she earned a college degree and stayed for many years. Returning to San Antonio in

By the outbreak of World War II, Tejanos generally possessed a sense of being of and from the United States and having certain basic rights as U.S. citizens. They were no longer a community of immigrants.

Macario García of Sugar Land, Texas, earned the Congressional Medal of Honor during World War II. Institute of Texan Cultures illustration no. 68-482

WORLD WAR II: WATERSHED. During World War II, Tejanos were drafted and sent overseas in large numbers. They fought along-side Anglos and received many honors. Five Mexican Texans were recognized with the Congressional Medal of Honor, the nation's highest award for heroism in war: Cleto Rodríguez, Silvestre Herrera, Macario García, Luciano Adams, and José M. López.

On the home front, Tejanos united to support the war effort. They purchased war bonds and trained as air-raid wardens. Children participated in patriotic drills. Mothers who had sons in the service formed groups such as the Victory War Mothers' Club. Members sewed clothes and gathered supplies to be shipped overseas.

Tejana women on the home front found new job opportunities open to them. Factories opened and expanded to produce war materials. Teenage girls attending trade schools switched from secretarial to engineering courses.[26] Women even worked as aircraft mechanics at Kelly Field in San Antonio.

When the servicemen returned home, most women left the technical jobs they had held during wartime. But women now had employment experience. Returning Tejano servicemen also brought new expectations. They had lived with Anglo comrades and gained familiarity with mainstream culture.

Like other veterans, Hispanic veterans qualified for benefits under the GI Bill. Many used it to pursue higher education. Veterans Administration loans made home ownership possible. Mexican Texans increasingly had funds to purchase middle-class consumer goods. World War II opened up pathways that ultimately led to school desegregation, political representation, and the Chicano movement of the 1970s.

In 1948 veteran Hector P. García organized the American GI Forum in Corpus Christi. Its original purpose was to assist Mexican American veterans in obtaining the federal benefits due them. Tejano veterans joined in large numbers.

The following year, a funeral home chapel in Three Rivers, Texas, refused to accept the body of a deceased Tejano veteran. Hector García and members of the GI Forum expressed outrage at this

the late 1960s, she was amazed to find herself hailed as "some sort of heroine."

Emma Tenayuca later earned a master's degree in education at Our Lady of the Lake University and taught in San Antonio public schools until retiring in 1982. She died of Alzheimer's disease in 1999.

Sources: Emma Tenayuca, address to the 12th Annual Conference of the National Association of Chicana and Chicano Studies, Austin, 1984, printed in *La Voz de Esperanza* 12, no. 7 (Sept., 1999): 4–5, 8–9; David Uhler, "Labor Activist Called City's Heroine," *San Antonio Express-News,* July 28, 1999, 1A, 8A; Emma Tenayuca, interview by Jerry Poyo, Institute of Texan Cultures Research Library, Oral History, Feb. 21, 1987.

▼▼▼

Esperanza Martínez overhauls an airplane engine alongside an Anglo coworker, Kelly Field, 1947. Institute of Texan Cultures illustration no. 3352-B

discrimination. They brought the situation to national attention and drew the support of Lyndon B. Johnson, then a United States senator from Texas. Through Johnson's intervention, Private Longoria was buried with military honors in Arlington National Cemetery near Washington, D.C.[27]

This incident enhanced the stature of the GI Forum and thrust it into the role of defending the rejected. Members pressed for other reforms of concern to Tejanos: voting, education, veterans' rights, and health care. The group joined forces with LULAC in mounting a ten-year legal struggle to desegregate Texas schools.[28]

THE FIFTIES: ERODING BARRIERS. The 1950s were an era of relative calm and prosperity. As people mounted legal challenges, the underpinnings of segregation began to tumble, but change came unevenly. In some areas, it was barely noticeable. Entrenched attitudes and other factors continued to limit opportunities for Tejanos and hamper their participation in public life.

The Korean Conflict drew young men away for military service. Senator Joseph McCarthy's campaign against communists chilled the open expression of opinions. Elaborate legal codes known as Jim Crow laws relegated African Americans to separate facilities. Jim Crow codes were applied informally to Mexican Texans as well. Restaurants posted signs that read "No Mexicans or dogs allowed." Movie house personnel directed Mexican customers to seats in the balcony. Families visiting parks were told to use "colored" drinking fountains.

Recalling his childhood, Lubbock resident Pete Pérez-Montalvo, a vocational instructor, told of being selected as a parade participant and the sting of rejection afterward: "One December a man from an Anglo church asked me to take part in a Christmas parade. I rode in a flatbed truck with a Black child and a Vietnamese. We sat looking at a globe with an open Bible in front of it. It was a very cold day when we paraded through downtown Lubbock. Afterwards he took us to a restaurant—this Anglo man with three minority children— but the restaurant wouldn't serve us. They sent us outside, and we had to sit on produce crates while they brought the food to us."[29]

While segregation persisted, job opportunities expanded. About three-quarters of Mexican Texans now lived in towns.[30] Advertisers courted their purchasing power. Banks began giving mortgages to families to buy homes. With veterans' preference in hiring, Tejano veterans secured jobs with military bases and other federal agencies, embarking on civil service careers.

The growing middle class understood education to be a key to advancement. Tejano parents sponsored back-to-school drives,

Spanish-speaking PTAs, community rallies, and king-and-queen balls. LULAC members instituted "Little School of the 400," a program that helped Tejano preschoolers learn four hundred basic English words before starting first grade. This later served as the model for the federal Head Start program.[31]

Under the state's English-only laws, schoolchildren were punished for speaking Spanish. One immigrant child, newly arrived with his family in 1954, felt bewildered by the treatment he received at an Eagle Pass school: "In the playground, I didn't know the rules. I was talking in Spanish to another kid. All of a sudden something hit me on the head. It was a big University of Texas ring that a man teacher had. He hit me real hard. I cried and cried, for I was a very small fourth grader."[32]

Many thousands of Mexicans crossed the Rio Grande during the war and postwar eras. Some people came legally under the bracero program that allowed for temporary "guest workers." Others arrived without the required documents. Nearly all immigrants came seeking jobs in Texas agriculture. Their sheer numbers and willingness to work kept farm wages low. Native-born Tejanos began to migrate farther away in search of higher income. Some families traveled as far as Michigan and Indiana before returning to Texas for the winter.

The trip to the harvests was grueling. Families rode together in the backs of trucks over bumpy roads. The drive could take several days. Towns had neither parking areas for trucks nor places where overnight travelers could bathe.

Sometimes a *troquero* (trucker) served as contractor, arranging the transportation and hiring workers for a grower. When they reached their destination, families first glimpsed their lodging, which might be nothing but a shed, shack, or barn. Migrant children attended school only during the winter months when there was no planting or harvesting to be done because families depended upon all members for their income.

Fieldwork was demanding and exhausting. Despite the hardships, workers recall acts of support for one another. In camps they

exchanged tips about growers, offered food, and played music. Josie Posada of Plainview, working as a child in the 1950s, remembers her father's upbeat spirit: "My dad would take us out of school before school ended. We'd go in April or May to Michigan to hoe beets. We were all working, all nine of us, out in the fields. We'd go home and we didn't even want to eat, 'cause we were too tired. But my dad would always treat us. . . . My dad would say, 'Where's the music?' He wanted us to be happy. He'd say, 'Come on, don't be so sad!' He'd put on the radio in the truck and start dancing with me or my sisters."[33]

With the influx of new immigrants, opponents called for de-

A migrant family heading north, San Antonio, 1946. Institute of Texan Cultures illustration no. 3225B

A mother and son await deportation inside a detention camp in McAllen, Texas, 1953. Institute of Texan Cultures illustration from box no. 4556

porting them. As in the 1930s, complaints circulated that Mexican workers stole jobs away from Americans, pushed down wages, spread diseases, and increased crime.

In 1954 the border patrol instituted "Operation Wetback." Officers swept through rural areas, arresting persons who lacked papers and returning them to Mexico. They also removed residents whose papers were suspect. Both LULAC and the GI Forum supported "Operation Wetback." Other Tejanos saw close friends or relatives uprooted and spoke out against the deportations.[34]

By the late 1950s, the political climate—both nationally and in Texas—had shifted. The liberal wing of the Democratic Party sent representatives to Washington like Lyndon Johnson and Ralph Yarborough, who did not favor Jim Crow segregation.

Increasingly, Tejanos campaigned for public office. Henry B. González of San Antonio won a seat in the Texas state senate in 1956, where he fought vigorously to block new segregation legislation. In 1957 Raymond Telles became the first Mexican American mayor of El Paso.

In the Supreme Court case of *Hernández v. Texas* in 1954, lawyers from LULAC and GI Forum argued that Mexican Americans were being unfairly excluded from Texas juries. The Supreme Court declared this practice unconstitutional. In addition, the justices found that Texas laws had discriminated against Mexican Americans as a class. Members of a class, like members of a race, had the right to equal protection under the U.S. Constitution.[35]

LULAC and GI Forum entered lawsuits against segregated schools. Court decisions in 1948 and 1957 forbade segregating Mexican American schoolchildren, but districts found ways to evade these orders, sometimes by classifying Tejano pupils as Caucasians and showing statistically that the Caucasian race suffered no discrimination. Additionally, school administrators combined Tejano and African American student populations to meet integration goals.[36]

The final four decades of the twentieth century saw increasing inclusion of Hispanics in all aspects of American life. For Mexican Texans, these changes were real but demanded ongoing struggle.

CHAPTER 4
The Late Twentieth Century

Identity in a Porous Society, 1960–2000

IN THE 1960 PRESIDENTIAL ELECTION, Mexican Texans mobilized to support the Democratic ticket. Their Viva Kennedy clubs were instrumental in John F. Kennedy's narrow win in Texas and in the nation. Kennedy disappointed supporters by failing to appoint Hispanics to federal positions. But Lyndon B. Johnson, who became president in 1963 after Kennedy's assassination, did so.

Johnson's Great Society initiative delivered federal programs and appointments to an extent previously unimagined. New laws removed obstacles to political participation. The poll tax was abolished in 1964. The federal Voting Rights Act of 1965 expanded opportunities for minority candidates. The Elementary and Secondary Education Act of 1965 brought a series of programs to bolster students identified as "disadvantaged": Head Start, Title I, and Migrant Education. The federal Bilingual Education Act of 1968 opened the door to bilingual instruction in Texas, long a goal of Tejano parents and educators. On the state level, the Texas legislature in 1969 quietly repealed the segregationist laws approved by that body from 1956 through 1957.[1]

Mexican Texans now had representation at the national level. In 1961 Henry B. González won a seat in the U.S. House of Representatives. Three years later, Eligio "Kika" de la Garza of South Texas joined him in the House. Emilio Abeyta, originally a priest and eventually

Valley farmworkers on the protest march to Austin, June, 1966. Institute of Texan Cultures illustration no. E-0012-064C

an attorney from the Texas Panhandle, was one of many Tejanos who secured a job in a federal program. As he explains, "My job there was to look for, recruit, hire, promote, award Hispanics working in all of these twenty-one legal divisions of the Department of Justice. . . . I was there in the halls of Congress when the Voting Rights Bill was being debated and when it was voted on. And it ultimately affected the smallest person in Slayton, because we now have bilingual ballots and now have bilingual people at the polls. . . . The government is *us*."[2]

Despite new job opportunities, some Mexican Texans desired change on a more fundamental level. They examined the philosophical underpinnings of U.S. society, raising issues of class and wealth. These younger activists were the seeds of the Chicano movement in Texas. For tactics, they turned to other movements sweeping the country in the 1960s, including the civil rights movement and efforts to end the war in Vietnam. They drew upon the examples of César Chávez, who was organizing farmworkers in California, and Reies López Tijerina, who led Mexican Americans in New Mexico.

▼▼▼

Following their successful Viva Kennedy campaign, Tejanos looked for ways to continue their political momentum. The GI Forum and several other groups came together to form the Political Association of Spanish-Speaking Organizations (PASSO) in 1961. From the start, the PASSO coalition faced disagreements between its moderate and more militant factions.

In 1963 PASSO joined with the Teamsters Union to bring about a political upset in Crystal City, a small town in Zavala County. Members conducted voter registration drives and organized cannery workers. Five Mexican Americans—from the town's poor and undereducated majority—filed as candidates for city council. All five defeated the incumbents in close elections. Crystal City's political establishment regained control in the election held two years later. Still, this incident disturbed political observers, for it showed that the Anglo power structure in South Texas could be broken.[3]

Tejano farmworkers, who earned barely enough to survive, learned of César Chávez's strikes in the vineyards of California. Following his example, Tejano field hands in 1966 mounted a series of wildcat strikes against melon growers in Starr County. Texas Rangers and local law enforcement officers ended the strikes. The farmworkers, undeterred, organized what became known as the Minimum Wage March. In June, 1966, they walked 290 miles from the Rio Grande Valley to Austin, cheered along the way by supporters from LULAC, GI Forum, and PASSO.

The Texas governor rejected their demands. Nonetheless, the Minimum Wage March energized support and an awareness of the farmworkers' plight. This event is generally regarded as the start of the Chicano movement in Texas.[4]

New, more confrontational groups arose that rejected blending into the dominant Anglo society and criticized Tejano organizations that promoted this. College students in San Antonio formed the Mexican American Youth Organization (MAYO) in 1967. They stressed pride in a culture extending back into pre-Hispanic times. For a symbol, they selected an Aztec warrior inside a circle. The group staged its first demonstration in front of the Alamo on July 4, 1967.

Although college students filled MAYO's ranks, the organization's ties were primarily to the grass roots. Most of the Hispanic students were members of the first generation in their families to enroll in college. MAYO also drew support from disaffected youth living in San Antonio's barrio and from urban and migrant workers throughout the state.

Under MAYO's encouragement, high school students initiated walkouts, pickets, and marches in numerous South Texas towns. They participated in protests at schools in Edcouch, Elsa, Weslaco, Del Rio, Uvalde, Laredo, Alice, Abilene, Kingsville, and Robstown, among others. Students pressed for bilingual-bicultural studies, more Mexican American teachers, and an end to discrimination in school-sponsored activities.[5]

At Edgewood High School, in San Antonio's predominantly Hispanic south side, students contended with run-down buildings and teachers who lacked certification. An Edgewood graduate explained the severity of the situation: "We had to wear our coats in winter; windows and doors were broken; the restrooms were never working."[6] In May, 1968, some three hundred Edgewood students left classes and staged a sit-in within the school's halls. They then marched carrying protest signs to the district's administrative headquarters five blocks away.

A few days later, concerned Edgewood parents met with Willie Velásquez, a local civil rights advocate, and a lawyer whom he had recruited. They drew up papers for a lawsuit contending that the system of funding public schools was unfair. By relying on property taxes for school costs, Texas was denying equal education to students who lived in poor districts. The case went to the U.S. Supreme Court where in 1973 the justices ruled in *San Antonio ISD v. Rodríguez* that the system of school finance did not violate the Constitution and that education is not a fundamental constitutional right. The ruling disappointed reformers in Texas, who had hoped to see the Constitution's equal protection clause applied to state school funding.[7]

In Crystal City, another dispute arose over the school policy for selecting cheerleaders. Tejano students and parents brought a list of grievances to the local school board. When the school board dismissed their petition, over two hundred students walked out of classes in December, 1969.

The strike soon spread from Crystal City High School to junior high and elementary schools. Over 65 percent of the students joined the protest. Parents brought meals to students who were picketing in front of schools. Mexican American tutors arrived in town to offer temporary classes. A student delegation traveled to Washington, D.C., to explain their grievances. After nearly a month, in January, 1970, the school board accepted most of the students' demands, and Crystal City's students returned to school.[8]

One of the participating students, who later became a high school teacher and city council member, described the lasting impact of the strike on her life: "Yes, we were hurt because we dared to stand up and speak up. But we were the light that showed the other places

Mothers and other volunteers serve food to striking students, Crystal City High School, December, 1969. Institute of Texan Cultures illustration no. 4148K

that there is a majority of Mexican Americans. . . . I was no longer embarrassed to eat my taco and my tortillas."[9]

MAYO members had supported and assisted the student strike. One of MAYO's founders, José Ángel Gutiérrez, was a native of Crystal City. Following the strike's success, Gutiérrez filed papers at Zavala County Courthouse to create a new political party, the Raza Unida Party. The party campaigned in the 1970 elections and won school board and city council posts in Crystal City, Cotulla, and Carrizo Springs.

Raza Unida's control of local government was most complete in Crystal City. With Gutiérrez at the helm, the group aggressively pursued federal money and instituted reforms including bilingual instruction, Chicano history courses, and a free school lunch program. Many Anglo parents withdrew their children from public schools or moved to other towns.[10]

By 1972 the Raza Unida Party was running candidates for statewide offices. Their candidate for lieutenant governor was a young Tejana woman, signaling that women were welcome in the party. The candidate for governor, Ramsey Muñiz, drew over 6 percent of the state's votes.

These stunning results established the Raza Unida Party (RUP) as an official third party with the right to appear on ballots. In the following years, RUP-backed candidates—both men and women—won local elections in Robstown, Kingsville, Pearsall, San Juan, Edcouch-Elsa, Eagle Pass, San Marcos, Lockhart, Hebbronville, and several small communities near El Paso.

By the mid-1970s, the movement's fortunes had turned. Internal strife and quarrels over leadership weakened RUP, as did negative press, legal attacks, and harassment by law enforcement officers. The governor of Texas denounced the party as a communist threat whose members were trying to turn Zavala County into a "little Cuba."[11]

The Chicano movement faded in Texas at a time when leftist movements were declining nationwide. Internal disunity and external hostility certainly played a role. But other factors were at work,

GANA RUP EL CONCILIO
Y LA MESA ESCOLAR: **CRISTAL**

VER PAG. 3

LA VERDAD
PUBLICACION QUINCENAL DE LA COMUNIDAD CHICANA

25¢

VOL. IV   NUM. 15   CRISTAL, Texas. AZTLAN   ABRIL DE 1974

vote may 4 JOSE ANGE
GUTIERRE
FOR COUNTY JUD

Fotografía: Industrias de Aztlán.

Raza Unida *newspaper promotes José Ángel Gutiérrez's campaign for county judge, April, 1974.* Courtesy of Vicente Carranzal

including the simple desire of many Mexican Texans for inclusion in American life. Calls for separatism did not appeal to individuals who saw the means at hand for "making it" within the system. Ironically, many of these opportunities had opened only through the legislative and confrontational efforts of activists. Some of the movement's causes, like bilingual education, were adopted by mainstream organizations and passed into law.

Henry B. González, Record-Setting Legislator

Henry B. González blazed a leadership trail and served as a role model to Tejanos who followed him in public life. His supporters remember him as a defender of the poor who always took time to hear the concerns of his constituents. "He went to my high school one time so we could see a real Hispanic political leader in our community. I remember one time he helped my mother get her retirement check. With him, all it took was a phone call."

Henry's parents emigrated from Mexico at the outbreak of the revolution in 1910. Henry was born in San Antonio in 1916. To support the growing family, his father took jobs in a drugstore, grocery store, and with the Spanish-language newspaper La Prensa.

Congressman Henry B. González meets with citizens in a department store, 1971. Institute of Texan Cultures illustration no. Z-2296A

The Chicano movement provided a training ground for future Tejano politicians and community leaders. Former MAYO and RUP members founded or promoted new advocacy organizations, including the Mexican American Legal Defense and Educational Fund (1968), Communities Organized for Public Service (1973), Southwest Voter Registration Education Project (1974), Mexican American Democrats (1976), El Paso Interreligious Sponsoring Organization (1980), and Valley Interfaith (1983).[12]

José Ángel Gutiérrez, who went on to become an attorney and political science professor, described the motivation that had compelled the young activists to take such daring stands. "If I stood face-to-face with the Rangers and looked them in the eye, my people were emboldened because they saw that I had no fear. Actually I was scared, but I couldn't let it show. . . . They called us subversives, radicals, militants, communists, drug dealers, thieves. We were none of those things. We were Mexicans trying to get a fair shake from the system."[13]

INCLUSION AND RETRENCHMENT, 1980–2000. The election of Ronald Reagan to the presidency in 1980 heralded a more conservative era politically, in both Texas and the nation. Many of the Great Society programs dating from the 1960s lost funding and came to an end. But by this time, Mexican Texans had taken advantage of federal grants and loans to enroll in college. The business and professional class increased considerably. By 1980 over 35 percent of employed Tejanos held professional office jobs, while another 35 percent practiced skilled trades. Less than 30 percent of Tejano workers engaged in unskilled jobs, mainly in the farm and service sectors.[14]

At the end of the twentieth century, people of Mexican descent worked as professors, public schoolteachers, doctors, lawyers, architects, engineers, bankers, scientists, social workers, news reporters, and law enforcement officers. Nearly every profession counted Mexican Americans among its members.

Prejudice was no longer acceptable in public discourse. Tejanos were viable political candidates and conducted successful campaigns. In 1981 Henry Cisneros won election as the first Tejano mayor of San Antonio since Juan Seguín in 1840. Like most of the new-style politicians, Cisneros emphasized building coalitions and avoided ethnic divisions.

Mexican Texans sat on school boards, city councils, and lower-level courts in towns throughout the state. Judith Zaffirini was elected in 1986 as the first Hispanic woman state senator. Tejana women earned the mayor's post in Kyle, Mercedes, El Paso, and Crystal City.

In 1990 Dan Morales became the first Hispanic attorney general of Texas. During his tenure, the Fifth Circuit Court ruled against the University of Texas Law School's affirmative action plan in *Hopwood v. Texas,* 1996. Morales interpreted this decision to end affirmative action in admissions to *all* Texas universities.

Tejano representation grew at the national level as well. In 1988, Lauro Cavazos, born on the King Ranch, was named U.S. Secretary of Education. President Clinton appointed Henry Cisneros as Secretary of the Department of Housing and Urban Development

In the 1930s young Henry enrolled in the University of Texas at Austin. To help pay for his education, he worked as a janitor in a dormitory and occasionally as a boxer in illegal matches. Afterward, he completed a law degree at St. Mary's University in San Antonio.

Henry B. González began his career with jobs as a probation officer, school social worker, and county housing director. In 1953 he was elected to the San Antonio City Council. In a contested election in 1956, he became the first Tejano in the Texas State Senate since Navarro in the nineteenth century.

González distinguished himself on the senate floor by a record-setting filibuster during which he spoke continuously for twenty-two hours against bills to expand segregation. Of sixteen proposals under

consideration, only two passed to become law.

After unsuccessfully campaigning to be Texas governor and a U.S. senator, González won a 1961 election to the U.S. House of Representatives—the first Mexican American ever to represent Texas there. At the swearing-in ceremony, he held in his free hand a bill to abolish the poll tax. The proposal became part of the Voting Rights Act of 1965.

González won eighteen consecutive elections and served in the House of Representatives for thirty-seven years. He lent his support to the Civil Rights Act, the Equal Opportunities Act, and President Johnson's Great Society legislation. He eventually became chair of the powerful House Banking, Finance, and Urban Affairs Committee.

(HUD). Tejanos held a wide range of political views and did not hesitate to challenge one another. In the 1992 elections, Henry Bonilla won a seat as a Republican to the U.S. House of Representatives— the first Tejano of his party ever elected to federal office. By the year 2000, fifteen Hispanics sat in the U.S. House of Representatives. Six of these fifteen Hispanics were from Texas.[15]

Amid political advances, Tejano parents continued to seek schools with more supportive learning environments for their children. Institutional segregation had ended in Texas, but many Hispanic children still attended underfunded and poorly equipped schools. The Mexican American Legal Defense and Educational Fund (MALDEF), working with the Edgewood School District, launched new lawsuits contesting the state system of funding public schools from property taxes. In 1989 the Texas Supreme Court issued a decision in the case of *Edgewood ISD v. Kirby.* The court ordered the state legislature to devise a fairer system, so that children in poor neighborhoods would receive the same spending per child as children in wealthy neighborhoods.

This decision was followed by a series of proposals, lawsuits, and appeals. The Texas Supreme Court in 1995 accepted a plan to transfer some tax monies from property-rich districts to property-poor districts. The plan, dubbed "Robin Hood" by its opponents, did make a difference. In 1968, when the first school-funding case was filed, Edgewood School District spent just $356 per student while nearby and wealthy Alamo Heights District spent $594 per student. Thirty years later, after the legal challenges, Edgewood had $5,390 to spend per student while Alamo Heights budgeted $5,232 per student.[16]

A Texas law passed in 1973 required school districts to provide second-language instruction to students who lacked the skills to comprehend English. Sporadic bilingual programs appeared, but they were limited to kindergarten through third grade. The goal was to transfer children to English-only classes as soon as possible. Some Mexican children were held back several years in first grade to learn English. MALDEF and the GI Forum filed suit criticizing these programs as inadequate. A district court judge in 1981 found that

▼▼▼

Mexican American students had suffered pervasive discrimination throughout the twentieth century—treatment that had produced "a deep sense of inferiority, cultural isolation, and sense of failure."[17] The judge ordered Texas to revamp and expand its bilingual program.

By the 1990s Tejanos saw more educational options become available. Most of the new efforts were for students identified as "educationally disadvantaged." Programs did not refer to Mexican Americans or any other ethnicity by name, but Tejano children were concentrated in low-income areas, where many of the programs began. Magnet schools in large cities accepted students with special interests like foreign language or fine arts. In the Lower Rio Grande Valley, amid great poverty, a network of "Alliance" schools set about building parental and community involvement in public schools. With the help of organizations like Southwest Industrial Areas Foundation Network and Valley Interfaith, the Alliance school program secured state funds.[18]

In San Antonio, a millionaire funded a foundation to provide vouchers to low-income students in Edgewood school district. With these vouchers, parents can pay tuition to enroll children in a private or parochial school. The ten-year, $50-million program began in 1998, drawing several hundred students away from Edgewood schools.

State funds to public schools depend upon the number of students enrolled. As Edgewood's enrollment dropped, so did its funding. Critics of the voucher program fear it will destroy public schools. Educational reform in Texas remains a contentious issue.[19]

Like other American workers, Tejanos have been deeply affected by globalization and other economic changes of recent years. In the 1980s manufacturing companies began to close plants in the United States. Some companies opened *maquiladoras* on the Mexican side of the border. *Maquiladoras* are tax-free, low-wage factories that operate with few environmental or labor restrictions.

With cheap labor available in Mexico, the garment industry in El Paso declined. Workshops opened, closed, and then reopened

González's liberal positions sometimes drew charges of communism. In 1963, when another legislator called him a "pinko," González chased him off the House floor. In 1986 González overheard a restaurant customer refer to him as a communist. The congressman, then seventy years old, punched him.

Citing principles, González took political positions where he stood almost alone, including calls for the impeachment of two successive presidents, Ronald Reagan in both 1983 and 1987 and George Bush in 1991. Looking back on his career, he noted, "In my time, I have had the honor to be vilified for standing up against segregation. I have had the privilege of being a thorn in the side of unprincipled privilege, and the great joy of being demonized by entrenched special interests."

In 1997 González suffered a dental infection that damaged his heart. Henry B. González died on November 28, 2000.

Sources: José Gómez, quoted in Joe Holley, "Encounters with a legend: San Antonians share tales of congressman"; "Henry B. González, 1916–2000"; Carmina Danini, "Legislator Leaves a Grand Legacy"; Bill Hendricks and Jaime Castillo, "Knuckle sandwich at eatery"; Henry B. González, quoted in "Henry B.'s legacy lives on," all in *San Antonio Express-News,* Nov. 29, 2000, section A.

under a new name to avoid paying wages. To defend exploited workers, El Paso native Cecilia Rodríguez formed La Mujer Obrera in 1982. The organization merged advocacy with mutual support. It offered a food bank, health clinic, and emergency social services program to help with the survival needs of its nine hundred members. Explained Rodríguez, "The majority of the workers are single mothers. They view a meeting as time they could be spending working to feed their kids. That's why we started the food cooperative, so they don't lose out by participating."[20]

In 1990 Mujer Obrera women chained themselves to their sewing machines to demand back wages. The U.S. Department of Labor investigated and found that more than $85,000 was owed to them.[21]

In 1990 the Levi Strauss Company announced that it was closing its Dockers clothing plant in San Antonio and relocating to Costa Rica. This caught its 1,150 employees by surprise. Of Levi's workers, 92 percent were Hispanic and 86 percent were women. Many had families to support. Earning an average wage of six dollars per hour, they had felt secure and even fortunate. Recalled Viola Cásares, "It was a shock to us because we had no warning at all. The man said that in order for them to stay competitive, they needed to shut down. In less than fifteen minutes, our lives were shattered."[22]

Discharged employees began to meet in a San Antonio church to discuss their situation. They found common ground as they shared stories of production quotas, workplace injuries, unpaid bonuses, and limited severance pay. Within a month, these women formed Fuerza Unida. They called for a nationwide boycott of Levi's products and filed a lawsuit. A federal judge rejected their suit in 1992, but Fuerza Unida continued to pressure Levi Strauss. During 1994 members took turns traveling to San Francisco and demonstrating in front of the corporate headquarters.

In 2000 Fuerza Unida still maintained an active presence in San Antonio. It now serves as an information clearinghouse that acts in solidarity with other worker movements in the United States and Latin America. Like Mujer Obrera, the group seeks to empower

▼▼▼

women. Fuerza Unida operates a sewing cooperative, food bank, and drop-in center for women in crisis. "Fuerza Unida made me see that I had rights I didn't even know I had," attests one participant.[23]

The North American Free Trade Agreement (NAFTA), passed by Congress in 1993, increased trade and traffic with Mexico. Border communities grew rapidly, straining the infrastructure of roads and public services. Additional factories closed and relocated, including Levi's plants in El Paso and the Lower Rio Grande Valley, leaving Mexican Texans out of work.

Military bases downsized as well in the new economy. Since World War II, the bases have been major employers of Tejanos and a gateway into the middle class. The most significant closure was Kelly Air Force Base in San Antonio, where closing was announced in 1995 and scheduled for completion in 2001.

Dressed in the style of the Mexican Revolution, Fuerza Unida garment workers pose as "Las Nuevas Revolucionarias," 1995. Courtesy of Fuerza Unida

Migrant men and children harvesting cherry tomatoes, Lower Rio Grande Valley, 1981. Institute of Texan Cultures illustration no. L-7090.71 Sheet 5, no. 13

Nearly twenty-five thousand employees reported to work at Kelly each day—by far the largest employer in the region. Hispanics comprised 61 percent of Kelly's workforce. Some were the second generation of their family to work there. They prospered by earning wages equal to the federal pay scale. Mexican Texans had advanced to the highest levels in the civil service hierarchy. "Many, many thousands were able to do what I did," said Edward García, who grew up on a peanut farm and eventually headed the Logistics Directorate. "Everyone here has an uncle, a daughter, a son who benefited from Kelly and all that prosperity."[24] Losing the base struck a blow to the extended community.

Efforts to tighten the U.S. border brought a military presence and wider-ranging border patrols. The U.S. Immigration Service uses high-tech equipment to capture Mexicans crossing the Rio Grande. El Paso built a wall along the riverbank to discourage illegal immigrants. Seeking to avoid capture, Mexicans look for more remote sections of the Rio Grande to attempt the crossing. Each year about three hundred undocumented persons drown while fording the river.[25] Others reach the United States but die from heat and exposure wandering in the Texas brushland. In 1987 eighteen stowaways in a train boxcar suffocated under the scorching summer sun near Sierra Blanca.[26]

Mexican Texans fill many of the border patrol jobs and bear responsibility for apprehending people who cross illegally. Other Tejano citizens shelter undocumented immigrants and provide legal and medical services to them. Tejanos assisted refugees during the sanctuary movement of the 1980s, when thousands of Central Americans fled civil wars in their countries.

Tejanos work actively in grassroots groups that seek to reduce poverty along the U.S.-Mexico border. Such organizations include Valley Interfaith in the Lower Rio Grande Valley and the El Paso Interreligious Sponsoring Organization (EPISO). These groups called attention to the desperate conditions in *colonias,* unregulated and unincorporated settlements just outside town boundaries. Developers sold small plots of land to low-income buyers, mostly Mexicans and Mexican Texans, with promises that utility lines and streets would soon follow. The promised services were not forthcoming, and the nearby town governments denied responsibility. Some purchasers erected shacks from materials like discarded wood and tin. Needing water, residents hauled it from distant wells. In some instances, water is stored in salvaged barrels that once held toxic chemicals. Dirt paths through colonia neighborhoods turn to mud after storms. Children suffer from dysentery, hepatitis, skin rashes, ringworm, and other ailments.

Community organizers have prevailed upon some border towns to incorporate colonias and extend utilities to them. They lobby state officials for bonds to bring water lines and sewer systems to colonias along the entire length of the border.[27]

Some migrant workers stay in colonias temporarily when they return to the Valley for winter. Texas' current farmworker population has greatly diminished—it consists today of perhaps fifty thousand persons.[28] Mechanization and urban growth have eliminated many farm jobs, while NAFTA gives agribusiness the flexibility to move elsewhere. A migrant mother in Pharr, whose youngest child has neurological disabilities, voiced concern after a futile job hunt. "Here in the Valley there is no help, no work—there is nothing."[29]

A few organizations continue to assist farmworkers, particularly the United Farm Workers Union and Texas Rural Legal Aid. State laws and regulations from the 1980s sought to remove certain dangers from the fields. One such law banned the short-handled hoe after farm workers strained their backs from using it. Growers were directed to provide drinking water, toilets, and hand-washing stations for field workers and to notify them when pesticides are sprayed. Children could no longer work when school was in session. In the 1990s the Texas legislature passed a law to link farm wages with the federal minimum wage. Even with these measures, farmwork in Texas remains a subsistence occupation.[30]

Conclusion

In today's world, Tejanos are interwoven in the fabric of American life. They hold jobs at all economic levels. In general, Tejanos of the business and professional class are weathering the economic changes brought by globalization. Blue-collar workers and farmworkers, however, face threats of displacement and increasing difficulties.

Social class has become the primary marker distinguishing groups of people. An individual's prestige or influence is determined more by social class than by race or ethnicity. Tejano professionals and entrepreneurs conduct themselves much like those of any other ethnic background. They expect and receive acceptance by their colleagues.

Ethnic distinctions have blurred. Anglo Americans eat Mexican foods, wear ethnic clothing, experiment with foreign customs, and adopt rituals and observances like Day of the Dead. A declining proportion of Tejanos speaks fluent Spanish. Even in the barrios, English is the language of everyday life. In San Antonio, nearly 70 percent of Spanish-surname households communicate in English as their primary language.[1]

Despite cultural blending, many Mexican Texans continue longstanding traditions, such as *quinceañeras* to celebrate a fifteen-year-old daughter's coming of age. They honor the Virgin of Guadalupe in the Catholic churches. Major cities and border towns hold civic events for *fiestas patrias*. Families gather at Christmastime to make tamales.

At Easter, Mexican Texans make *cascarones,* brightly colored eggshells filled with confetti. The tradition began in the 1860s when Carlota, the wife of Mexico's Emperor Maximilian, brought fancy eggshells from France to serve as perfume containers. The Mexican people replaced the perfume with small pieces of paper and filled

Tamales

Practically every Tejano has grown up eating tamales as winter approaches. Women gathered in the kitchen chatting while preparing dozens of tamales. Making tamales was a social experience that was practiced in November when it was cold enough for butchering. Today, most families have a favorite store where they purchase a couple of dozen tamales already made.

In the distant past, preparations began by boiling a hog's head and feet with lots of garlic and salt. While the meat boiled, the women prepared corn husks and masa dough.

1 medium pork roast
1 clove garlic
dash of salt
4 tablespoons red
  chili powder
4 cups masa harina
2 tablespoons
  shortening or lard

Quinceañera, *San Antonio, 1969. Zintgraff Collection.* Institute of Texan Cultures illustration no. Z-317

the empty eggshells at Easter to symbolize Christ rising from the tomb. Although the custom of breaking "eggs" or *cascarones* on someone's head has died out in Mexico, it remains a mischievous tradition in South Texas.

Preparing for a new exhibit, staff of the Institute of Texan Cultures posed a question to visitors: "Are there customs and traits that

Selena Quintanilla Pérez, 1971–95. Institute of Texan Cultures illustration no. L-1991-11-12

1 teaspoon salt
1 cup hot water
30–40 corn husks

1. Boil pork roast with garlic and salt until well cooked. Shred meat and mix with chili powder.

2. For dough, mix masa harina, *shortening or lard, and salt. After shortening is cut into the size of tiny peas, add hot water; use more water if needed to make thick dough.*

3. Wet and soak corn husks until flexible and rip off a long thin strip for tying.

4. Spread dough on wet corn husk. Put a small spoonful of the meat mixture in the middle of dough, wrap husk around it, and tie with thin strip of corn husk.

5. Steam in large pan with boiling water for 45–60 minutes.

Source: Katherine S. Kirlin and Thomas N. Kirlin, *Smithsonian Folklife Cookbook* (Washington, D.C.: Smithsonian Institution Press, 1991), p. 28.

▼▼▼

bind Tejanos together?" Their answers reveal a deep-seated, abiding identity:

- Love of life! A zest for living happily, even in the midst of poverty or want. Respect for mothers, fathers, and especially grandparents and great-grandparents.
- Family comes first. The value of family united no matter what happens.
- Making tamales and *menudo* with my grandma at Christmas and *buñuelos* at New Year.
- Foods—those brought by ancestors from Mexico and made over or done differently because of the Texan influence.
- *Quinceañeras;* having *arras* at your wedding, tamales at Christmas.
- Bonds between *compadres* and *comadres* after sponsorship of a baptism, confirmation, first communion, or wedding.
- Music—*conjuntos* with their instruments such as the accordion. *Bajo sexto* and the rhythms from indigenous, American, and European roots.
- Music plays a great part in our lives.
- The Roman Catholic tradition.
- We are not *all* Catholic—some of us have never been that, but religious heritage is important.
- Family is very important, and never forgetting our roots, who we are, what our foods are, and keeping our traditions alive.[2]

In 1995 the Tejano singing star Selena, age 23, was killed by the president of her fan club. Her death sparked a statewide outpouring of grief, vigils, and memorials. Selena Quintanilla Pérez, like other contemporary Tejanos, moved between and expressed the two cultures. She merged aspects of her Mexican heritage with life in mainstream America. Her stage presence was sensual, yet she extolled

▼▼▼

family values, traveling to singing engagements with her family. She was English-language dominant until her teens and then studied to improve her Spanish. Despite attaining wealth, she lived in a working-class neighborhood in Corpus Christi.[3]

Today's Mexican Texans claim a proud heritage and strong sense of group identity. They work to fulfill their lives in a society they have helped to nurture, create, and energize. While many still struggle in poverty, others have achieved prestige and affluence. Mexican Texans have affirmed their place in the history of Texas. Describing their legacy, individuals proclaim:

- We are a strong, proud race full of ambition and courage.
- We care for each other and the strides we have made together.
- Being bilingual and bicultural makes a person richer.
- [We] worked just as hard as everybody else, picking cotton and produce in the hot sun.
- Our Spanish and Indian ancestors accomplished much more than the pitifully few items in the history books.
- We are loyal, hard-working, loving, patriotic *Americans.*
- Tejanos have been successful members of the community and have a right to be recognized and honored.
- We must be proud of who we are and where we came from and pass knowledge from our heritage on to our children and brothers and sisters so that we will not be forgotten.[4]

Notes

INTRODUCTION

1. José Vasconcelos, "La Raza Cósmica" (1925), cited in Victor Mejia, "Mestizaje and Self-Hate," http://www.geocities.com/itzliehecatl/mestizaje.html (Apr. 3, 2003).

CHAPTER 1. ESTABLISHING ROOTS: THE COLONIAL ERA, 1519–1821

1. Laura González, from a visitor survey at the Institute of Texan Cultures, Mar. 28, 1995.

2. "The Narrative of the Expedition of Coronado by Pedro de Castañeda," in *Spanish Explorers in the Southern United States, 1528–1543*, ed. Frederick W. Hodge (1907; reprint edition, New York: Barnes & Noble, Inc., 1965), pp. 362–63.

3. Letter of Fray Damian Massenet to Don Carlos de Sigüenza (1960), tomo 17 (ms. 54), doc. 13, in Archivo de Ministerio de Asuntos Exteriores, Madrid, translation adapted from *Spanish Exploration in the Southwest, 1542–1706*, ed. Herbert Eugene Bolton (1908; reprint edition, New York: Barnes & Noble, Inc., 1967), p. 359. Spanish original is available on microfilm at San Antonio Missions National Park.

4. Letter of Fray Damian Massenet to Don Carlos de Sigüenza, author's translation.

5. "Itinerary of the De León Expedition of 1689," in *Spanish Exploration*, ed. Bolton, p. 398.

6. Letter of Don Juan de Olivan Rebolledo, Dec. 24, 1717, Bexar Archives, Center for American History, University of Texas at Austin, author's translation.

7. "Diario y Derrotero de Domingo Ramón," 1716, Archivo General de la Nación de México, Center for American History, University of Texas at Austin, author's translation.

8. Fray Benito Fernández de Santa Ana to Gov. Tomás Felipe Winthuisen, June, 1741, in *Letters and Memorials of the Father Presidente Fray Benito Fernández de Santa Ana, 1736–1754*, ed. Fr. Benedict Leutenegger, Documentary Series No. 6 (San Antonio: Old Spanish Missions Historical Research Library, Our Lady of the Lake University, 1981), p. 42, author's translation.

9. Citizens' petition to the town council of San Fernando de Béxar, Nov. 13, 1797, Archivo de la Secretaria del Estado de Coahuila-Saltillo, Legojo 8, Expediente

491, trans. Dora Elizondo Guerra; copy available at Catholic Archives of Texas, Austin.

10.	Bando of Governor Manuel Muñoz, July 31, 1795, in Jesús F. de la Teja, *San Antonio de Béxar: A Community on New Spain's Northern Frontier,* Albuquerque: University of New Mexico, 1995, p. 109.

11.	*Guidelines for a Texas Mission: Instructions for the Missionary of Mission Concepción in San Antonio, 1787,* in Documents Relating to the Old Spanish Missions of Texas, vol. 1, trans. Fr. Benedict Leutenegger (San Antonio: Old Spanish Missions Historical Research Library, Our Lady of the Lake University, 1994), p. 37.

12.	Fr. Joseph Mariano Cárdenas, "Inventory of Mission Espíritu Santo de Zuñiga, November 27, 1783," ed. and trans. William H. Oberste, document at Goliad State Historical Park (1980), p. 18. Spanish original is available on microfilm at Old Spanish Missions Historical Research Library, Our Lady of the Lake University, San Antonio.

13.	*Guidelines for a Texas Mission,* pp. 17, 35.

14.	"Report of Fr. Gaspar J. Solis, 1768," in *The San José Papers, Part 1, 1719–1791,* trans. Fr. Benedict Leutenegger (San Antonio: Old Spanish Missions Historical Research Library, Our Lady of the Lake University, 1978), p. 149.

15.	*Guidelines for a Texas Mission,* p. 37.

16.	Cárdenas, "Inventory of Mission Espíritu," pp. 26–27.

17.	Gov. Manuel Salcedo, "Report on Four San Antonio Missions, June 19, 1809," in *The San José Papers, Part II, August 1791–June 1809,* trans. Fr. Benedict Leutenegger (San Antonio: Old Spanish Missions Historical Research Library, Our Lady of the Lake University, 1983), pp. 276–77.

18.	King of Spain to the Viceroy, the Marquis of Las Amarillas, June 30, 1775, cited by Charles Wilson Hackett, "Policy of the Spanish Crown Regarding French Encroachment from Louisiana, 1721–1762," in *New Spain and the Anglo-American West: Historical Contributions Presented to Herbert Eugene Bolton,* vol. 1 (New York: Kraus Reprint Co., 1969), p. 137.

19.	Domingo Cabello, Governor of Texas, decree at San Antonio de Béxar, June 24, 1781, trans. Dora Elizondo Guerra, cited in Frank W. Jennings, *San Antonio: The Story of an Enchanted City* (San Antonio: *San Antonio Express-News,* 1998), pp. 199–200.

20.	Jesús F. de la Teja and John Wheat, "Béxar: Profile of a Tejano Community, 1820–1832," in *Tejano Origins in Eighteenth-Century San Antonio,* ed. Gerald E. Poyo and Gilberto M. Hinojosa (San Antonio: University of Texas Institute of Texan Cultures, 1991), p. 4.

21.	Gerald E. Poyo, "Immigrants and Integration in Late Eighteenth-Century Béxar," in *Tejano Origins,* p. 86.

▼▼▼

CHAPTER 2. WEATHERING A CENTURY OF CHANGE, 1800–1900

1. Andrés Tijerina, "Under the Mexican Flag," in *Tejano Journey, 1770–1850,* ed. Gerald E. Poyo, (Austin: University of Texas Press, 1996), p. 44.

2. Goliad Ayuntamiento to State Congress, January 15, 1833, Nacogdoches Archives Transcripts, Center for American History, University of Texas at Austin, cited in Poyo, *Tejano Journey,* p. 45.

3. Jean Louis Berlandier, *Journey to Mexico during the Years 1826 to 1834* (Austin: Texas State Historical Association, 1980), 2:291 [1828], cited in Timothy M. Matovina, *Tejano Religion and Ethnicity in San Antonio, 1821–1860* (Austin: University of Texas Press, 1995), p. 11.

4. José María Sánchez, "A Trip to Texas in 1828," ed. Carlos E. Castañeda, *Southwestern Historical Quarterly* 29, no. 4 (Apr., 1926): 283, cited in Poyo, *Tejano Journey,* p. 35.

5. José María Rodríguez, *Rodríguez Memoirs of Early Texas* (1913; reprint edition, San Antonio: Standard Printing Co., 1961), pp. 8–9.

6. Eulalia Yorba, "Another Story of the Alamo," *San Antonio Express,* Apr. 12, 1896, p. 13, cited in Timothy M. Matovina, *The Alamo Remembered: Tejano Accounts and Perspectives* (Austin: University of Texas Press, 1995), pp. 54–55.

7. Antonio Menchaca, "Memoirs," Center for American History, University of Texas at Austin, p. 80, cited in Stephen L. Hardin, "Efficient in the Cause," in Poyo, *Tejano Journey,* p. 60.

8. Arnoldo De León, *The Tejano Community, 1836–1900,* (Albuquerque: University of New Mexico Press, 1982), p. 28.

9. W. Eugene Hollon and Ruth Lapham Butler, eds., *William Bollaert's Texas* (Norman: University of Oklahoma Press, 1956), 230 [1843], cited in Timothy M. Matovina, "Between Two Worlds," in Poyo, *Tejano Journey,* pp. 84–85.

10. Mary Maverick to Agatha S. Adams, Aug. 25, 1838, cited in Matovina, *Tejano Religion and Ethnicity,* p. 38.

11. Jean Marie Odin to Jean-Baptiste Etienne, June 17, 1842, Catholic Archives of Texas, Austin, cited in Matovina, *Tejano Religion and Ethnicity,* p. 30.

12. William Barret Travis to Jesse Grimes, Mar. 3, 1836, in *The Papers of the Texas Revolution, 1835–1836,* vol. 4, ed. John H. Jenkins (Austin: Presidential Press, 1973), p. 502.

13. Córdova Rebellion papers, 1838, Nacogdoches County Court Records, Special Collections of Ralph W. Steen Library, Stephen F. Austin University, trans. Jesús F. de la Teja, cited in Paul D. Lack, "The Córdova Revolt," in Poyo, *Tejano Journey,* p. 97.

14. Lack, "The Córdova Revolt," p. 108.

15. "The Autobiography of George W. Smith," *Southwestern Historical Quarterly* 34 (Jan., 1933): 202, cited in De León, *Tejano Community,* p. 13.

16. Matovina, *Tejano Religion and Ethnicity,* p. 44.

17. David Woodman, *Guide to Texas Emigrants* (Boston: M. Hawes, 1835), pp. 60–61, cited in De León, *Tejano Community,* pp. 54–55.

18. U.S. Congress, House, *Difficulties on the Southwestern Frontier,* H. Exec. Doc. 52, 36th Cong., 1st sess., Mar. 20, 1860, pp. 80–81, cited in David Montejano, *Anglos and Mexicans in the Making of Texas, 1836–1986,* p. 32.

19. Arnoldo De León, *Mexican Americans in Texas: A Brief History,* 2d ed. (Wheeling, Ill.: Harlan Davidson, Inc., 1999), p. 39.

20. Ibid., p. 19; De León, *Tejano Community,* pp. 18–19.

21. *El Paso Herald,* July 21, 1898, p. 4, cited in De León, *Tejano Community,* pp. 68, 77.

22. *San Antonio Express,* May 4, 1892, p. 2, in De León, *Tejano Community,* p. 196.

CHAPTER 3. IN THE MATRIX OF MODERN TEXAS, 1900–1960

1. De León, *Mexican Americans in Texas,* p. 66.

2. Ibid., p. 83; David Montejano, *Anglos and Mexicans in the Making of Texas, 1836–1986* (Austin: University of Texas Press, 1987), p. 192.

3. Dimmit County grower quoted in Paul Taylor, "Mexican Labor in the United States: Dimmit County, Winter Garden District, South Texas," *University of California Publications in Economics* 6, no. 5 (1930): 441, cited in Montejano, *Anglos and Mexicans,* p. 193.

4. Montejano, *Anglos and Mexicans,* p. 160.

5. Ibid., p. 242.

6. Andrés Sáenz, "Rancho El Fresnillo," family history manuscript, San Antonio, Institute of Texan Cultures, 1996, p. 39.

7. De León, *Mexican Americans in Texas,* p. 92.

8. Américo Paredes, *With a Pistol in His Hand* (Austin: University of Texas Press, 1958), pp. 159–61.

9. Montejano, *Anglos and Mexicans,* pp. 119, 125.

10. San Antonio Department of Health, *Annual Report* (1937), cited in Julia Kirk Blackwelder, *Women of the Depression: Caste and Culture in San Antonio, 1929–1939* (College Station: Texas A&M University Press, 1984), p. 112.

11. San Antonio Department of Health, *Annual Report* (1936), p. 5, cited in Blackwelder, *Women of the Depression,* pp. 178–79.

12. Blackwelder, *Women of the Depression,* pp. 106–107.

13. Ibid., pp. 98, 104–105, 141.

14. *El Paso Times,* Nov., 1934, cited in Yolanda Chávez Leyva, "Faithful Hard-Working Mexican Hands: Mexicana Workers During the Great Depression," *Perspectives in Mexican American Studies* 5 (Tucson: University of Arizona Mexican American Studies & Research Center, 1995): 71.

▼▼▼

15. De León, *Mexican Americans in Texas,* p. 104.

16. Ibid., p. 96; "Mexican Americans and Repatriation," *The Handbook of Texas Online,* http://www.tsha.utexas.edu/handbook/online/articles/view/MM/pqmyk.html (Jan. 24, 2002), hereinafter cited as *HOT Online.*

17. De León, *Mexican Americans in Texas,* p. 100.

18. Ibid., p. 102.

19. Ibid., p. 100; Blackwelder, *Women of the Depression,* pp. 111, 117.

20. Blackwelder, *Women of the Depression,* pp. 109, 124.

21. Ibid., pp. 132–35; De León, *Mexican Americans in Texas,* pp. 106–107.

22. Blackwelder, *Women of the Depression,* pp. 138–39.

23. Ibid., pp. 104–105, 143.

24. Details of the pecan strike are from ibid., 141–45, 148–49; "Pecan-Shellers' Strike," *HOT Online,* http://www.tsha.edu/handbook/online/articles/view/PP/oep1.html (Jan. 22, 2002).

25. *El Paso Times,* Sept., 1933, cited in Leyva, "Faithful Hard-Working Mexican Hands," p. 71.

26. *San Antonio Light,* Mar. 29, 1942.

27. De León, *Mexican Americans in Texas,* p. 116; "Felix Longoria Affair," *HOT Online,* http://www/tsha.utexas.edu/handbook/online/articles/view/FF/vef1.html (Jan., 25, 2002).

28. "American G.I. Forum of Texas," *HOT Online,* http://www.tsha.utexas.edu/handbook/online/articles/view/AA/voa1.html (Jan. 25, 2002); "Mexican-American Organizations," *HOT Online,* http://www.tsha.utexas.edu/handbook/online/articles/view/MM/vzmvj.html (Jan. 25, 2002); *"Delgado v. Bastrop Independent School District,"* *HOT Online,* http://www.tsha.edu/handbook/online/articles/view/DD/jrd1.html (Jan. 25, 2002).

29. Community meeting for Tejano project, audiotape transcription by the author, St. Joseph's Church, Lubbock, Tex., Oct. 16, 1994, Institute of Texan Cultures Oral History Program, San Antonio.

30. Manuel Peña, *The Texas Mexican Conjunto: A History of Working-Class Music* (Austin: University of Texas Press, 1985), p. 128, cited in De León, *Mexican Americans in Texas,* p. 111.

31. De León, *Mexican Americans in Texas,* p. 118; "Little School of the 400," *HOT Online,* http://www.tsha.utexas.edu/handbook/online/articles/view/LL/kdl2.html (Jan. 30, 2002).

32. Pete Pérez-Montalvo, community meeting for Tejano project, audiotape transcription by the author, St. Joseph's Church, Lubbock, Tex., Oct. 16, 1994, Institute of Texan Cultures Oral History Program, San Antonio.

33. Josie Posada, video interview by the author, Plainview, Tex., Apr. 8, 1999, Tejano exhibit archives, Institute of Texan Cultures, San Antonio.

34. De León, *Mexican Americans in Texas,* pp. 119–20; "Operation Wetback," *HOT Online,* http://www.tsha.utexas.edu/handbook/online/articles/view/OO/pqo1.html (Jan. 25, 2002).

▼▼▼

35. *"Hernández v. State of Texas,"* *HOT Online,* http://www.tsha.utexas.edu/handbook/online/articles/view/HH/jrh1.html (Jan. 25, 2002).

36. For information on segregation in Texas schools, see "Segregation," *HOT Online,* http://www.tsha.utexas.edu/handbook/online/articles/view/SS/pks1.html (Jan. 29, 2002); "Civil-Rights Movement," *HOT Online,* http://www.tsha.utexas.edu/handbook/online/articles/view/CC/pkcfl.html (Feb. 6, 2002); "Mexican-American Organizations," http://www.tsha.utexas.edu/handbook/online/articles/view/MM/vzmvj.html; De León, *Mexican Americans in Texas,* pp. 117–18.

CHAPTER 4. THE LATE TWENTIETH CENTURY: IDENTITY IN A POROUS SOCIETY, 1960–2000

1. For political changes during this period, see Montejano, *Anglos and Mexicans,* pp. 278, 286; De León, *Mexican Americans in Texas,* p. 125; "Mexican-American Organizations," http://www.tsha.utexas.edu/handbook/online/articles/view/MM/vzmvj.html; "Bilingual Education," *HOT Online,* http://www.tsha.utexas.edu/handbook/online/articles/view/BB/khb2.html (Jan. 30, 2002).

2. Emilio Abeyta, video interview by the author, Lubbock, Tex., Apr. 6, 1999, Tejano exhibit archives, Institute of Texan Cultures, San Antonio.

3. "Crystal City Revolts," *HOT Online,* http://www.tsha.utexas.edu/handbook/online/articles/view/CC/wmc1.html (Feb. 4, 2002); Montejano, *Anglos and Mexicans,* pp. 282, 284.

4. De León, *Mexican Americans in Texas,* pp. 127, 138; Montejano, *Anglos and Mexicans,* p. 284.

5. For more about MAYO, see "Mexican American Youth Organization," *HOT Online,* http://www.tsha.utexas.edu/handbook/online/articles/view/MM/wem1.html (Feb. 4, 2002); De León, *Mexican Americans in Texas,* pp. 130–31; Montejano, *Anglos and Mexicans,* p. 284.

6. Linda Bononcini, 1967 Edgewood graduate, quoted in "Troubled Edgewood on edge of cultural cliff again," *San Antonio Express-News,* July 27, 1998, 6A.

7. For information about Edgewood protest and lawsuit, see "Edgewood's on the edge again," *San Antonio Express-News,* July 27, 1998, 1A, 6A; "Protest changed school funding," *San Antonio Express-News,* July 27, 1998, 7A; "30 years later, loss still pains Edgewood lawyer," *San Antonio Express-News,* July 28, 1998, 1A, 4A; "Man devotes career to school-fund fight," *San Antonio Express-News,* July 29, 1998, 1A, 8A.

8. For more about the Crystal City school walkout, see "Crystal City Revolts," http://www.tsha.utexas.edu/handbook/online/articles/view/CC/wmc1.html; "Before there was clout, there was Raza Unida," *San Antonio Express-News,* Sept., 2000, 10A; De León, *Mexican Americans in Texas,* pp. 131–32.

9. Severita Lara De La Fuente, quoted in "Crystal City walkout seen as turning point," *San Antonio Express-News,* Dec. 6, 1994, 10B.

10. "Crystal City, TX," *HOT Online,* http://www.tsha.utexas.edu/handbook/

online/articles/view/CC/hfc17.html (Feb. 5, 2002); De León, *Mexican Americans in Texas*, p. 132.

11.   De León, *Mexican Americans in Texas*, p. 135.

12.   "Tejano Politics," *HOT Online*, http://www.tsha.utexas.edu/handbook/ online/articles/view/TT/wmtkn.html (Jan. 25, 2002); Montejano, *Anglos and Mexicans*, pp. 290–91.

13.   José Ángel Gutiérrez, quoted in Lawrence Clayton and Susan C. Allen, "Looking Back at Crystal City," *Texas Journal of Ideas, History and Culture* 20, no. 1 (fall–winter, 1997): 42, 43.

14.   Montejano, *Anglos and Mexicans*, p. 299.

15.   For political representation, see "Tejano Politics," http://www.tsha. utexas.edu/handbook/online/articles/view/TT/wmtkn.html; De León, *Mexican Americans in Texas*, pp. 143–44; "Mexican-American Women," *HOT Online*, http:// www.tsha.utexas.edu/handbook/online/articles/view/MM/pwmly.html (Feb. 6, 2002); "San Antonian, a thorn to GOP," *San Antonio Express-News*, Nov. 29, 2000, 8A; "Breaking barriers," *San Antonio Express-News*, July 3, 2001, 4A.

16.   "Edgewood's on the edge again," 1A, 6A; "Man devotes career to school-fund fight," 1A, 8A.

17.   Judge William W. Justice, *United States v. Texas*, 1981, quoted in "Bilingual Education," http://www.tsha.utexas.edu/handbook/online/articles/view/BB/ khb2.html (Jan. 30, 2002).

18.   Geoff Rips, "A Quiet Revolution," *The Texas Observer* 92, no. 7 (Apr. 14, 2000): 15.

19.   For the school voucher program in San Antonio, see ibid., p. 19; "Parents applaud voucher benefits," *San Antonio Express-News*, Aug. 9, 1998, 1A, 8A; "Declining enrollment edges district to new challenges," *San Antonio Express-News*, July 30, 1998, 4A.

20.   Cecilia Rodríguez, quoted in "Women strikers put heat on sweatshop king," *The Guardian* 29 (May, 1991): 7.

21.   Ibid.

22.   Viola Cásares, quoted in "Former Levi workers recall plant's closing," *San Antonio Express-News*, Mar. 4, 1999, 1B.

23.   Juanita Reyna, "Let There Be Change," *AFSC*, Newsletter of American Friends Service Committee, Texas-Arkansas-Oklahoma, 10, no. 3 (Oct., 1997): 5. Other sources for Fuerza Unida information are "Hilo de La Justicia," campaign bulletin of Fuerza Unida, spring, 1998; "Ex-Workers Take on Levi Strauss," *San Francisco Chronicle*, July 18, 1994, 1A; "Ex-Levi workers to appeal ruling," *San Antonio Light*, Mar. 13 1992, 1A; "A Thousand Lives," series of five special reports appearing in the *San Antonio Light*, Nov. 11–15 1990.

24.   Quote and statistics from "Kelly meant a prosperous life for Hispanics," *San Antonio Express-News*, Apr. 21, 2001, 1A, 14A.

25.   "Bodies of Rio Grande drowning victims hard to identify," *San Antonio Express-News*, Aug. 2, 1998, 15A.

▼▼▼

26. Boxcar incident in "Coyotes deal in human cargo," *San Antonio Express-News*, Aug. 2, 1988, 15A. Other information about immigrants' fates in "Perilous journey," *San Antonio Express-News*, Aug. 2, 1998, 1A, 14A; "Death lurks below surface of tranquil Rio Grande," *San Antonio Express-News*, Nov. 24, 1996, 14A.

27. "Colonia," *HOT Online*, http://www.tsha.utexas.edu/handbook/online/articles/view/CC/poc3.html (Feb. 6, 2002); Rips, "A Quiet Revolution," pp. 15–16.

28. De León, *Mexican Americans in Texas*, p. 148.

29. María Guadalupe Ortiz, video interview by Patti Elizondo and the author, Feb. 26, 1999, San Juan, Tex., Phyllis McKenzie, trans., Tejano exhibit archives, Institute of Texan Cultures, San Antonio.

30. De León, *Mexican Americans in Texas*, pp. 147–48.

CONCLUSION

1. Neilsen survey in "Debate raises issues of Spanish," *San Antonio Express-News*, Feb. 10, 2002, 16A.

2. Anonymous written comments submitted at visitor feedback station, first-phase Tejano installation, Institute of Texan Cultures, San Antonio, Apr.–Oct., 1995.

3. Information about Selena in De Léon, *Mexican Americans in Texas*, p. 149; "Quintanilla Pérez, Selena," *HOT Online*, http://www.tsha.utexas.edu/handbook/online/articles/view/QQ/fquxg.html (Jan. 25, 2002).

4. Anonymous written comments submitted at visitor feedback station, first-phase Tejano installation, Institute of Texan Cultures, San Antonio, Apr.–Oct., 1995.

Selected Bibliography

Chipman, Donald E., and Harriett Denise Joseph. *Notable Men and Women of Spanish Texas*. Austin: University of Texas Press, 1999.

de la Teja, Jesús Frank. *San Antonio de Béxar: A Community on New Spain's Northern Frontier*. Albuquerque: University of New Mexico Press, 1995.

De León, Arnoldo. *Mexican Americans in Texas: A Brief History*. 2d ed. Wheeling, Ill.: Harlan Davidson, Inc., 1999.

———. *The Tejano Community, 1836–1900*. Albuquerque: University of New Mexico Press, 1982.

Montejano, David. *Anglos and Mexicans in the Making of Texas, 1836–1986*. Austin: University of Texas Press, 1987.

Poyo, Gerald E., ed. *Tejano Journey, 1770–1850*. Austin: University of Texas Press, 1996.

Index

Page numbers in *italics* refer to illustrations and captions.

▼▼▼

▼▼▼

▼▼▼

▼▼▼